A spiritual optic nerve that will consciously optimize the way we look at any of our daily situations, and how we relate to them while being attentive of our uniquely made chemical composition: *Dr. Allen Zali Cizungu, Vancouver, Canada.*

Another rare insight, a moving life testimony, an unforgettable story that can inspire us Christians for eternity: *Pastor Vim Fourie, Yeoville Christian Center, Johannesburg, South Africa.*

THE REALITY OF OUR CHEMICAL COMPOSITION AND OUR SPIRITUALITY

THE OVERLOOKED FACTS

B.N. Dunn

WestBow
PRESS
A DIVISION OF THOMAS NELSON

Copyright © 2012 B.N. Dunn

All rights reserved. No part of this book may be used or reproduced by any means, graphic, electronic, or mechanical, including photocopying, recording, taping or by any information storage retrieval system without the written permission of the publisher except in the case of brief quotations embodied in critical articles and reviews.

Editing by:
Editor World LLC
PO Box 24
Newport, VA 24128
United States

WestBow Press books may be ordered through booksellers or by contacting:

WestBow Press
A Division of Thomas Nelson
1663 Liberty Drive
Bloomington, IN 47403
www.westbowpress.com
1-(866) 928-1240

Because of the dynamic nature of the Internet, any web addresses or links contained in this book may have changed since publication and may no longer be valid. The views expressed in this work are solely those of the author and do not necessarily reflect the views of the publisher, and the publisher hereby disclaims any responsibility for them.

Certain stock imagery © Thinkstock.
Any people depicted in stock imagery provided by Thinkstock are models, and such images are being used for illustrative purposes only.

ISBN: 978-1-4497-5348-1 (sc)
ISBN: 978-1-4497-5349-8 (hc)
ISBN: 978-1-4497-5347-4 (e)

Library of Congress Control Number: 2012909059

Printed in the United States of America

WestBow Press rev. date: 06/14/2012

To my siblings, and my beloved mother whom the eyes of time hid from me for so long.

CONTENTS

Acknowledgments ix
Preface xi

PART I: WHY DID I DENY GOD? 1
Chapter 1:   Memoir of the Pain that Knitted Me 3
Chapter 2:   The Coin Maker 39
Chapter 3:   The Turning Point 49

PART II: OUR REALITY REDEFINED 63
Chapter 4:   Reality Redefined 65
Chapter 5:   The Revelation of Life and Death 91
Chapter 6:   The Expresive Style of the Bible 101
Chapter 7:   Transmutation into the Story of all Revelations.... 105
Chapter 8:   The Power of the Eden's Curse on us................... 130
Chapter 9:   Hunted by the Shadow of Desire 139
Chapter 10: Our Actions Versus Our Desire and Their
             Reality Implications 143
Chapter 11: The Begining of Restoration at Babel 152
Chapter 12: Abraham's Essence 161
Chapter 13: The Impossible Made Possible............................. 165
Chapter 14: The Essence of Atonement 176
Chapter 15: The Essence of the Messiah 180
Chapter 16: Success Versus Our Reality 187
Glossary 205
About The Author... 207

ACKNOWLEDGMENTS

I give special thanks to my beloved wife Cynthia and my two kids Reish-ka and Tobe, whose presence has filled years of emotional emptiness, and finally help me to reclaim myself. My thanks go also to Brad and Candice, who came into my life not just to encourage and inspire me, but also to be my life itself. Doctor Stella Dogun who gave the beauty that framed this work, and Doctor Oluchi Ozumba reminded me not to dream in French. I thank Grant Flaum, Steve Gooch, and the members of Central Park Church for their unflagging support in giving me a vision even when I felt that there were no way out of life. To New Covenant Church in Bryanston, South Africa, my first spiritual home, I offer my gratitude. Many thanks as well go to all those who have been supportive of me while waiting patiently for the completion of a project they felt to be theirs.

PREFACE

As a young man living in the war-torn Democratic Republic of Congo, known then as Zaire, growing up was like going through the horror of a crashing airplane with a minimal chance of survival before landing in puberty. I experienced not just the daily challenge of facing the equatorial heat with my bare feet while trying to flee ricocheting bullets, but also the excruciating realization that an empty stomach would be an accomplice in ending the lives of many, something that the bullets did not do. The heavy rain swept the frail but still living, defenseless and starving bodies away during their attempts to cross the rivers and sink some of them into the deep to be food for alligators, thus rendering their efforts in running away from bullets wasted. Hidden from the world, these frightful events happened in African's second largest country, world's eighteenth most populous nation, which is almost a quarter of the size of the United States of America.

It was through the lens of this great nation's reality and its impoverished people that I happened to accumulate some isolated impressions related to the cause and effect of circumstances that were plaguing me in particular and the world in general, and then to correlate them with the idea of an existing, loving God that so many people profess.

The object of "the Reality of Our Chemical Composition and Our Spirituality" is to furnish you with a complete, self-contained understanding of today's reality and the God factor in a coherent, deep-thinking style. However, it is also a piece that I hope will challenge your knowledge and bring about an understanding of systematic concepts of your personal life experience as never laid out before in any conventional Christian book.

During my many years as an atheist, I was often confronted with a simple glimpse at the splendor of the evidences concerning a divinity that were so deeply woven into the texture of thousands of believers' minds. As it was previously engrained in me, however, these ideas of a spiritual being had always seemed so absurd that their explanations did not fill the wide gap initiated by myriad logical questions regarding our actual reality, and in particular, mine. The word "God" itself appeared then to express in a simple and convenient form the characteristic of a blind pursuit of customs. It merely meant to me that such a word was confined within prescribed limits as is the life of a human being. At that time I thought, how would someone "believe" in a God whose presence is absurd and limited to reason? At a very young age I had hated the idea of a God, but deep inside I was scared that one might exist; to convince myself otherwise, I had to prove that the idea was irrational. It was during this journey of hate that I discovered the "Desire Story." I made it my priority to look for a logical reason for events and for the desire of man to seek a divinity in which I rarely believed. After several years of intense search for the truth, I finally learned the art of transmutation into the world realities that helped me attain understanding through inspiring experiences that stretched me within and beyond the borders of my native land.

Because "the Reality of Our Chemical Composition and Our Spirituality" is a blend of the manner in which my educational and atheistic background collided with the Christian reality that was dawning inside me, its contents will focus primarily on key Bible passages that inspired me, and their wisdom as gleaned through the lens of my personal life experiences.

"The Reality of Our Chemical Composition and Our Spirituality" goes beyond the shell of words to send its readers into the very clouds of blissful wisdom, unlike any average Bible based book ever written before. Though it might be a controversial book to some theologians or conservative Christians, I would like it to be viewed more as a symbiosis stemming from a transition from an extreme denial to an extreme expressive acceptance of Jesus Christ. Before tinting the next pages of this book with some deep-thinking principles that guided me in acknowledging God's existence, I thought it worthwhile to use this juncture to take you back to the genesis of my childhood, gathered from a palpable, painful past that cost me almost everything.

PART I:
WHY DID I DENY GOD?

Chapter 1

Memoir of the Pain that Knitted Me

"How can I believe in a God who wasn't even there and did nothing to prevent all this, if of course He was there?" I screamed at two women preaching to me on a car parking lot.

What was I doing on a car parking lot? What was it that God should have prevented? And foremost, how did these two women end up preaching to me?

I was born in the 80s in the African great lakes region of the Democratic Republic of Congo, formerly called "Zaïre." It is home to four major ethnic groups and two hundred and fifty smaller tribes.

My country is known not only for its colossal size, but also for the fact that it is endowed with myriad precious natural resources, as among them diamonds, gold, cobalt, copper, manganese, petroleum, uranium and columbite-tantalite (coltan), used to manufacture capacitors. It is from its uranium of Shinkolobwe that the Manhattan Project culminated in the making of the first atomic bomb that claimed the lives of thousands of men, women and children living in the Japanese cities of Hiroshima and Nagasaki.

Although a giant in terms of natural resources of all kinds, yet the Democratic Republic of the Congo remains a dwarf with respect to its social and political life. Its population still lives in nearly inconceivable misery, as though it was the poorest developing nation in the world. The situation in my family was not exceptional.

Sheltered by the blurry reflection of its own shadow, my small town of Kolwezi was a beautiful mining city situated along the legendary Lualaba River, the largest headstream of the majestic Congo River. The undulating reddish hills carpeted with man-made gullies and the lavish tropical trees shared the landscape of this little metropolis and its history. Shunned for its size, yet it is in this part of my country that the famous copper mining company "La Generale des Carrières et des mines" (La GECAMINES in short) had the largest concentrations of copper and cobalt. Thus, extraction mines were everywhere.

The city of Kolwezi was created by Western powers with the intent to establish it as the headquarters for their mining activities in Zaire. The majority of laborers who occupied high positions as engineers in these mines were Kasaians, people who came from a central eastern tribe of Zaire. They were the descendants of first Kasaians who had been brought from Kasai province in 1906 to work for the Union of mines of High Katanga (UMHK). Thus, they attended the company's sponsored schools and colleges. Another group of Kasaians voluntarily immigrated in the early 1960s in search of greener pasture.

"*My father*," Martin, and a few of his buddies happened to be among those who settled in mid-1960s, but ended up working in other sectors of economy, such as education, health and finance. It was later in the 1970 that he became a Latin philosophy teacher at "Ukweli" High School situated near the mine of Manika. "Ukweli" is a Swahili word meaning the truth.

"*My mother,*" Julienne, was, as most women there, a housewife who had strong beliefs in the supernatural powers of her dead ancestors to protect the family's wellbeing. Her ancestors were to her like roots are to a tree; she could not root them out without jeopardizing her own survival. One of her practices was to spill a few drops of water or some food crumbs on the ground before a meal to honor the dead ancestors she believed to be her providers. She advised me sometimes as the eldest son in my family, not to copy everything from Western culture. "All they want son, is to have you worship their crucified Jesus who has nothing to do with your daily life, and thus make you ignore the suffering of your ancestors who died in the slave-ships, in the sugar cane and cotton fields, whipped and left to bleed to death," she said. "'You are your ancestor's blood spatter, the result of an injury, the breath of a long fight, born in silence and without insult.' 'Please, son, do not ever betray the memory of those who made who you and I are today,'" she would go on insisting.

Despite the economic hardships we faced, our household was blissful though there are always emotional strains in every family.

"*My only sibling, my younger sister,*" Patricia, had a slight disability, in which her right leg was growing more slowly than her left. This condition was named: Limb length discrepancy (LLD), and in her case, it began when she was still a toddler and received an improperly-injected malaria shot. The injection destroyed the muscle tissues around the bone.

As the years went by, Patricia and I both grew mentally and physically stronger as siblings; we both attended the same school, where everyone, including our teachers, knew us as two outstanding and well-disciplined children. My parents were both gifted with a natural love for their children, to the extent that their caring was well-known in our neighborhood.

Our family's size was constrained because our mother was not allowed to give birth for the first five years of my parent's marriage due to gynecological problems about which I never learned the details."

My childhood recollections were tinted with many wonderful surprise visits from family friends and relatives, but none of them left such a great impact as the visit of one of my uncles, Denis Tshowa, who came from the country's largest city, Lubumbashi. He was also employed in the same mining company as a "cadre," French for a "senior executive" in a well-known school in downtown Lubumbashi. His rare kindness to us was to be a path that later guided our lost and wandering minds to their ordained serenity.

If you approached the intimidating silhouette of our town from the distance, you would hear loud noises from the copper and cobalt factories, where heavy engines, trucks, cars, and even the popular two-wheeled bicycles named "Kinga" were all in motion. Kinga bicycles were designed to transport goods all over the country anywhere the roads were in poor condition or where trucks and cars could not pass. This constant cacophony reminded you how busy people were preoccupied with completing their daily routines.

Your first sight early in the morning, when the little town yawned and stretched to life, was that of a paradise where a tropical breeze, humid and soothing blended with the songs of birds. Everything was wrapped in a foggy-smoky sunbeam just to prepare your mind to a beautiful enjoyable day that was unfolding ahead of you. Most main roads in the center of the city of Kolwezi were asphalted, but regular township streets were of red clay along which school buses, heavy mining trucks, private cars and pedestrians jostled each other in an atmosphere filled with dust in order to get to their destination on time.

The population was multicultural, as in much of the country, with all social classes and ethnicities featured. I knew that my father was an atheist who never believed in any spiritual being called "God." According to him, it was man himself who was at the center of what he believes and could selfishly use these beliefs to shape others to their detriment. Man created the term "God" through his own imagination to enslave his fellow man who is already apprehensive about a kind of revenge that he defined to be God's only. Just the fact that my father saw the way in which a man treats his fellow human being today, in his view, if man had the power to own the oxygen, he would have taken it all for himself and let everyone else asphyxiate.

He would always share with us, his children, the dual facets of the human mind which are responsible for what he summarized to be "a constructive destruction."

At our young ages we did not understand well his philosophy's views. He did not even allow us to sit next to anyone, whether at home, in church or on a public street, if that person was preaching about God and "His existence," for fear that we would embrace the concept of God and limit our own inquisitive minds. Patricia and I were sometimes spanked or even beaten severely if we "swear to God;" an expression that was common among children at that time, used to assure their friends to believe in what they want to tell them.

Whenever other kids talked to us about God and the possibility of going to hell and burning there forever, we would both go home crying with fear that God would one day destroy our family. This attitude of fear really irritated my father. He would make us sit while he explained to us relentlessly how the idea of a Divinity came about. For him, the idea of a divinity was a capitalist conspiracy used to advance its political agenda of exploiting the laborers through imposition of the Christian faith. In this way, the possibility of emancipating human's minds through education would be subverted in service to their interests as long as men were kept in a state of mortal fear. The Torah, which is a part referred to by Christians as the Old Testament, says that a Jew can keep a slave, but a Jew kept as a slave must be redeemed, and that is how God and religion become a false, empty, and foolish justification for exploiting innocent people. He drummed his beliefs into me and my sister daily, adding beatings to his tutelage if one of us so much as exclaimed unconsciously, "Oh my God!"

What was very conflicting about his assessments and opinions was the fact that he would sometimes identify himself and all tribesmen of Kasai province as the Jews of Africa. The reason behind this contradictory statement was due to the fact that the Lubas of Kasai, called "Kasaians," have sometimes considered themselves to be the Jews of Africa because they believe they prevail over the country's intellectuals and consider themselves to be professional entrepreneurs of the Jewish caliber. The Belgians cultivated them as laborers, not as administrators of the colonial order. But with time, Kasaian families were housed in the mining company's up-class city; their children were educated in company-built schools and colleges, and this prepared them to be ready to infiltrate to the top, through even the most oppressive regimes both before and after independence of the Congo. By then, the Kasaians themselves were seen as the instruments of oppression but no matter what happened, they always managed to reach the top.

My father was a Jew by virtue of oppression, not by his race or a character that trusted in a God who exists. He would make us watch his favorite movie, "Escape from Sobibor," the 1987 film about two hundred and fifty-thousands Jews who were murdered in a concentration camp in Poland, and the three hundred who lived to escape in October 14, 1943.

For me, this movie was a sufficient piece of evidence that man is at the center of human calamity. He is the creator of world events, whether those are good or evil, and the idea of a God was a fantasy designed to fill gaps in our knowledge when confronted with challenges that we could neither understand nor change.

At our ages, these philosophical thoughts were like a dialogue that my sister Patricia and I had to recite verbatim without any comprehension of their true essence and meaning.

When I turned ten years in 1990, my father was impressed by my command of his philosophy of life. My attitude moved him to make a choice that would forever change my life. He enrolled me in a special school of philosophy for children with special gifts so that they could learn the "oratory arts." This would enable the student to acquire the skills of public speaking and applied rhetoric. The whole purpose was that I should be able to graduate younger as an autodidact and proceed to University as a gifted and eloquent law school student. His vision was deemed possible even if I had to spend the next eight years of internship at Kolwezi diocese. It was there that I met "Magistère," which means "he who has the authority of teaching," i.e., the big Master.

Magistère was a seventy-two year old Belgian named Van Neer Gustave from the Salesians order of Catholic pontifical congregation called Don Bosco or the Society of St. Francis de Sales. I was advised by my father to detach myself from the religious teachings that would be used for career purposes only, and not to build my virtue on them. I befriended two boys of my age, Gervé and Gabain, who lived a life of character and principle. With his curly hair, Gervé was known for his straightforwardness and humbleness. He believed that he could multiply himself a thousand-fold whenever he would taste different things. For Gabain, any man who said he has never been a happy person in his life may at least become one through his friends' or relatives' happiness, but envy deprives him of this last resource.

I visited my family once every weekend to get my clothes washed and eat my favorite home-cooked meals. By then it seemed that things were not going well in the country. There were waves of political unrests that exalted a climate of corruption. The self-acclaimed military marshal, Mobutu Sese Seko, who then was the president of the Congo, was becoming unpopular within his single party government "Movement populaire de la Révolution" (MPR)—the Popular Movement for Revolution. Mobutu was a dictator who had ruthlessly ruled Congo that he later renamed "Zaire," for almost three decades without organizing a single election. All Congolese were members of his MPR by the time they were born.

On April 24, 1990, Mobutu Sese Seko, the Leopard King of Zaire, decided to declare an end to his MPR single-party rule and authorize the beginning of a multiparty government that would pave the road to democracy through a transitional government. This move was triggered by his fear in watching on the international news as his best friend, Nicolae Ceausescu, the president of Romania, was assassinated in a court session broadcast in December of 1989. By that time the Cold War was cooling and the Berlin Wall had recently fallen; Mobutu's Western supporters: the United States, France, and Belgium, had withdrawn their support by 1990. This, together with mounting strikes and demonstrations in Kinshasa and elsewhere, compelled Mobutu to open a "sovereign national conference" to facilitate a national dialogue between different parties and his authoritarian government. Many opposition leaders returned after years in exile and multiple opposition parties mushroomed in the space of just twenty-four hours, including the media that had long been banned. The students of the University of Lubumbashi in the province of Shaba currently named Katanga, where I resided grasped the opportunity to convey their long-suppressed thoughts about the single-party regime. But in a matter of just a few weeks, unknown commandos nicknamed "les Hiboux,"—"the Night Owls," were sent to the campus at night to massacre students. They carried out murders and abductions of many students whose fate still remains unknown.

The Night Owls were well trained to terrorize at night only those who openly expressed their antagonism towards the Mobutu regime. No one was spared, from women and children, to the dogs roaming the street; the latter were used sometimes to convey some of the hostile messages against the regime, by dressing them in western suits and ties that were banned by Mobutu in his attempt to purge the country of all colonial and western cultural influences.

Teachers went unpaid for almost fifteen years, and the deferred pay they finally received was less than ten U.S. dollars per month. Soldiers and police now hid at night around trees and large water ducts and made it their practice to arrest anyone walking at night, and charge him with the trumped-up offense of "instigating night trepidation on state agents on patrol;" an offense that carries a penalty of two cups of strong coffee or a maximum of one night in police cells.

In September of 1991, these harassments culminated in devastating looting of shops by unpaid soldiers and the hungry population all across the country. More than a hundred people were killed in the process; most of those who died were poisoned by stolen goods that they believed were edible foods. Illiteracy was a contributory factor in this type of death. Amazingly and shamelessly, the looted goods were resold by the soldiers on the streets and still no one was arrested or prosecuted.

The aftermath of the looting paralyzed the small business sector, and this resulted in thousands of middle-class people being laid off. A great famine ravaged the country, and the province most affected was the one in which I lived, the province of Katanga.

For the first time in my life I noticed a major change in our refrigerator. I was accustomed to opening its doors whenever I was home on the weekend to serve myself from a variety of food in it. Now, I was confronted with a lunch of cold corn meal porridge with nothing else inside than salt. My mom was not at home, but out on the street trying to sell a few household items to generate cash for "Fufu."

"Fufu" is the main daily West African meal, usually made from cassava, yams, and sometimes mixed with coconut yams, plantains, or maize. In the capital Kinshasa, it is mostly made from boiled cassava and unripe plantain beaten together. Currently, these products are made into powder or flour and can be mixed with boiling water to obtain the final product while eliminating the onerous task of beating it in a mortar with a pestle.

However, in politics things were much worse. The major opposition parties came up with a coalition movement called "Union Sacrée de l'Opposition Radicale"—the Sacred Union of Radical Opposition—that was to create a transition government. A politician known for his long anti-Mobutu position, Mr. Étienne Tshisekedi, originally a native of the Kasai tribe, was designated as the person to lead the transitional government to the first democratic election. Tshisekedi was sworn in as Prime Minister on October 16, 1991 with Mobutu's approval, but he only lasted for a week and was sacked by Mobutu. Tshisekedi nicknamed Sphinx of Limete, gained the support of Western governments, and sought control over Zaire's Central Bank. With that prospect, Mobutu was frightened because control of the printing and distribution of money was the indispensable means by which he not only enriched himself, but also supported his cronies and bribed his enemies. Yet, even without the central bank in his control, Tshisekedi received support from the major business men from his native province of Kasai who enriched themselves with diamond trafficking; thus, this helped the Union Sacrée to remain strong. Mobutu became increasingly frustrated; something had to be done to bring the opposition to its knees. Mobutu reversed the game by bringing back the two acclaimed politicians from Shaba Province: Jean Nguza Karl-i-Bond and Gabriel Kyungu wa Kumwanza.

But who were these two personalities in the Zairian politics?

Nguza was not a new card in the political arena of the great Zaire; he had been a foreign minister in Mobutu's government in the early 1970s. He then became the political director of Zaire's single political party, the MPR. In 1977 he was accused of attempting to seduce the first lady, charged with treason and sentenced to the death penalty, which was never carried out. It was reported that he was physically tortured by the insertion of a metal tube into his urethra, through which jets of air were introduced, causing the blood vessels to rupture, as well as the application of electrical shocks to his testicles. But a year later he was freed by presidential pardon and then became Prime Minister. Two years later, after serving as prime minister, Mr. Nguza then fled into exile in Belgium, where he wrote a book entitled "Mobutu l' incarnation du Mal Zairois"—"Mobutu the incarnation of Zairians Evil"—which exposed the breadth and depth of Mobutu's corrupt government. He later testified in U.S. Congressional hearing in Washington, D.C. about Mobutu's illegal fortune. Then, incredibly, after all that, Mobutu forgave him yet again and called him back to the country just to appoint him as Zaire's ambassador to Washington. Two years later, he became Foreign Minister again. Nguza was an educated politician who had received a master's degree in international relations from the Catholic University of Leuven in Belgium. Still Mobutu was able to mold him like clay in the hands of the master political potter that he was.

In 1991 Nguza was out once more and heading the "Union des Fédéralistes et des Republicains Indépendants" (UFERI) —"Union of

Federalists and Independent Republicans"—which was one of the three main opposition parties in the Sacred Union of Radical Opposition.

The other principal player and close ally of Nguza, Gabriel Kyungu, appeared more credible than Nguza as an antagonist to Mobutu. Kyungu together with Tshisekedi, had given a blistering public criticism of Mobutu's government in 1980. The two were jailed and tortured. Kyungu was one of the first public figures to denounce the massacre of students at the University of Lubumbashi (UNILU) by the Night Owls commandos, drawing large crowds with his propagandist speeches. He was the one who coined the "Hibou" term (Night Owl) to describe the assassins sent at night to massacre civilians. In ancient Rome, the Owl is considered the bird of a bad omen, presaging death; Caesar's murder was announced by the screeching of owls. In Africa, the same is applied, the bird is sometimes associated with death or witchcraft in Africa, so the term "Hibou" was analogous to what the soldiers were there to do in the silence of darkness: to bring death.

Mr. Nguza and even Kyungu were nonetheless bribed by Mobutu, who was looking for a way to weaken the opposition of the Union Sacrée. In November of 1991, they decided to detach their party UFERI from the Union Sacrée; Mobutu seized that opportunity immediately and appointed Nguza as the Prime Minister of the country, replacing Tshisekedi; Kyungu was appointed the governor of Katanga.

With Kyungu's arrival in Katanga, his native province, the hostilities against Kasaians (Luba of Kasai) began. With the sole purpose of weakening the opposition of Tshisekedi, who was greatly supported by his tribal people (Kasaians), governor Kyungu launched a campaign known as "Debout Katanga!" —"Rise up, Katanga!"—Without delay. Its slogan was "Katanga Ni Ya Bakatangais" "Katanga belongs to the people of Katanga only."

In a series of public insults and radio speeches, Kyungu vilified Kasaians residing in Katanga by claiming them to be responsible for the misery of the Katangese population. He would call them "Wadudu" (Swahili for "insects"). The Kasaians were unexpectedly called foreigners in their own country and thought of as a tribe driven by selfishness, one that left its diamond-enriched region to invade the Katangese land. For Kyungu, every Kasaian living in Katanga and especially in the headquarters of the Katanga mines (Kolwezi) should have his belly moistened with oil and be given a push in order to help him slide smoothly on the train tracks for a four hundred mile trip back to his native province. "The Kasaians must go and then the Katangese should have their nice jobs and nice houses back," he said.

In order to carry out an action long planned by Mobutu, Kyungu created the Juferi, a youth brigade in his party, as a street-fighting army. Most of them were unemployed, illiterate thugs from rural villages. Juferi mobs were sometimes provided with gasoline to set houses afire, and with beer and marijuana to stoke their aggression. But all these violent acts were at that time carried in remote areas on the outskirts of Kolwezi and other minor towns of Katanga.

On January 16, 1992, hundreds of thousands of people marched through the streets of Kinshasa, a thousand miles away from Katanga Province in support of the national conference on democracy, which Nguza, through Mobutu instigation, had ordered closed. Mobutu's personal guards, the GSP, which stands for "Special Presidential Guards," opened fire on the marchers on the streets of the capital; then Mobutu himself fabricated evidence to blame Nguza for ordering it closed; then soon afterward Mobutu himself allowed the national conference to resume. In August, the National conference nominated Tshisekedi to be Prime Minister once more. Kasaians in Katanga celebrated his nomination but it was rumored that some of them mockingly chanted through the streets of Lubumbashi with leashed dogs that wore ties and tags stating Nguza and Kyungu. This act was considered a great offense to the Katangese community, which unleashed an unprecedented attack by Juferi mobs called "Operation Pononayi" —"Operation beat them up". The Juferi were also reported to have bathed themselves in a type of black magic formula called "Bizaba" to protect themselves in case Kasaians retaliated this time. But this attack was repressed due to some political tactical maneuver that might have worked against them. However, later that same night, in a meeting held on the square of Kolwezi, the Governor Kyungu called the Katangese to hunt the Kasaians working in Gecamines and forcefully evict them by taking their offices and positions in the company. A month later, on February 16, 1992, the militiamen of Juferi with the assistance of the national gendarmes, and in complicity with the municipal and provincial authorities, embarked on a campaign of persecution and forced displacement of the Kasaians living in Kolwezi.

Armed with canes, gasoline, machetes, and AK47s, they snapped in a way that had never happened before. It was the extreme loud noise of gun shots that alerted our instructor to the fact that something ominous was happening in the city. In the blink of an eye, the whole beautiful town of Kolwezi was wrapped in a cloud of dark smoke. In these types of situations, it is advisable to let the intern students go to their homes so that they can be together with their respective families. As we were heading to classes at about seven in the morning, unaware of what was going on, we were met in the hallway by Magistère, father Van Neer, who had an expression on his face of grave concern.

"Bonjour Magistère," we all greeted him in French: "Good morning master."

"Oh! Mes élèves, c'est pas une bonne matinée, y a un ça ne vas pas," he replied in rapid informal French: "Oh, my students, it's not a good morning, there is something wrong."

"Il n'y peut qu'avoir un ça ne vas pas si un prêtre pédophile obstrue trois élèves qui se dirigent calmement aux cours ce que tu n'es pas je pense," a classmate responded amusingly: "It can only be wrong if a pedophile priest blocks passage to three students walking calmly to the classroom, which I believe you are not."

"Gervé, je ne blague pas et je t'apprend à être un orateur public pas un injurieur d'insolence public," he angrily reprimanded him: "Gervé, I am not being playful, and I am teaching you to be a public speaker, not a public disrespectful insulter."

"Mes excuses Magistère, c'était une blague," Gervé replied humbly: "My apologies Master, it was a joke."

It was the first time that Magistère had reacted this harshly to jokes about pedophile priests, a subject that permeated his speech whenever he spoke of "hell" and those who would be burnt in it.

After pulling himself together, he stared steadily at each one of us and demanded that we take a few of our clothes in plastic bags that we could carry around easily in case things turned out to be fine and we needed to come back to school, but for the moment we needed first to go to our families. The distance from school to our residences was half an hour's walk. The only school bus we had was not available on that day, and waiting would not have guaranteed its arrival. After walking for about twenty minutes, we heard a loud deafening noise, the next thing we saw was a mushroom-shaped cloud of smoke rising over the tops of the mango trees.

Gervé and my other friend Gabain were nowhere to be seen. I had unconsciously tumbled on the ground at the time of the thundering noise. As I was still trying to figure out what was happening, I was struck at the same time with a great fear triggered by the fact that I was left alone without my friends. Like one mentally retarded, I stood by watching running dogs, and confused fowl, as though they were the ones responsible for what I had just experienced. Moved by an inner spirit of survival, my eyes swiveled through the smoky space, trying to make sense of the blurry scene that was unfolding just a few feet away. My consciousness was revived by the sight of a severely-bleeding man passing by with both of his ears cut. This spectacle made me realize that I was in a truly deadly zone, and if I wanted to get out of it, I had to move as quickly as I could to get home to my family. But as I pushed my way deep into the little town, hoping to find my beloved family, the whistling of AK47 bullets and other heavy weapons hampered my progress. Disoriented, I stood at a familiar bus station called "Mushibi," trying hard to suppress my fear while looking around hoping to see my family. My eyes caught sight of a second gruesome scene, that of an infant one or two years old crying next to her dead mother, whose belly was split open, while tens of thousands of people carrying luggage on their heads raced by heading to the train station. Nevertheless, this scene would not have stopped me from pressing my way into town to unite with my family had not a man grabbed me by the arm.

Due to the fact that I was touched by an unknown man holding a machete, my adrenaline surge so suddenly that I urinated in my pants. This man is going to slice me into pieces, I thought to myself.

"Hey little boy where do you think you're going?" He asked me in Swahili, with a weird look emphasized by a Hitler-style mustache.

"Please don't kill me, I will do everything you ask me to, just don't take my life," I begged him feverishly.

"I am not here to take your life but to save it. Keep moving before they find us here," he said, dragging me with all his force. I did not even have time to pick up my plastic bag that contained the few clothes that Magistère had told us to take home with us. I had dropped it in panic when the man first grabbed my arm. I did not ask him any question if not just responding to his. He had a massive, intimidating, muscular body structure.

"Where do you come from?" he asked me.

"I am from Manika," I replied, sounding almost as if I was short of breath.

"I mean what tribe are you from?" He asked the question explicitly.

"I am a Luba from Kasai," I answered his question truthfully.

"I knew it, I could tell...blood of the same ancestors' clicks sometimes," he replied.

He then looked down as though trying to be sure that I understood what he meant, and said to me: "My child, no one from Kasai is left alive in this town, the few of us who made it are all going to the train station. If you had taken another few steps into the city you would be dead by now like all these people." He pointed his index finger at a nearby shallow pit where a young man's head was decapitated with a machete and pounded with a pestle. A few inches away his motionless body lay in the street. It looked like he was murdered not long before we walked by, as we could see his blood still flowing out near a drain. It was as though people who were committing these awful murders were enjoying seeing another human being in agony. They had used their victims' blood as ink to write on the ground their slogan "Katanga Ni Ya Bakatangais"

In order to better express the degree of the revulsion engraved on their hearts against Kasaians, Juferi mobs would attack married Kasai women of any age and demand that they deny their own tribal husbands before raping and killing them in public. It was as though all their sadism was part of a pleasurable ritual, and that such rituals would help them win their cause.

Arriving at the train station, I shuddered, and then fell on the ground in frozen silence. My frail body was violently sick from the dreadfulness of those gruesome sights, which weighed too heavily on both my mind and its consciousness. These were scenes of human cruelty that I was unable to chase from my mind. At eleven years of age, this was a bad way to start my early adolescence, an introduction that exposes the evil that people are capable of perpetrating against their fellows, humans no different from them except by virtue of being of another tribe.

As I came to my senses, the old man, like an alien from another planet, was gone without a word. I was left there alone in the midst of an amazing multitude of people.

Almost sixty percent of Kasaians made it to the train station with all that they could carry. I, with absolutely nothing but the clothes I wore, was hoping that somewhere among the crowd, I would find my parents and my sister Patricia safe and sound. But there were just too many people scattered along the train station, some having severe injuries that completely disfigured their faces and blinded them, making it difficult for people to identify each other. Night was falling rapidly as it does anywhere near the equator and it was becoming almost impossible to search for my family. Sitting on the edge of a road close by, I was fighting sleep, exhausted by the trauma I had just experienced. I reminisced, having slept for only a couple of minutes due to the blowing cold and driest wind that I had ever felt. It was as though winter was setting its claws in my heart, surely a heart loaded with so much pain. To be alive at that moment was cruel; I could no longer believe in the smile of a human being, and the sun could no longer shine with enough warmth to melt the ice of my pain. It did not matter anymore to me if the flame of my life was extinguished right there in that cold night. Looking into the dark, I thought of the silence of churches, and the evidence of the existence of God all being analogues to the void of obscurity surrounding me. On that day I trusted my father's words: "Man, he alone created the idea of God."

At nine the following morning, a train was sent to carry everyone away to Mwene Ditu, a suburban city in Kasai Oriental. We were crammed in like sardines: young men, young ladies, old women, children, babies, suitcases, stinking shoes, dishes, fowl, goats and all of us ready for a three day slow trip to the central East province of Kasai.

The journey itself turned into a tragedy. I recall two passengers who became involved in a terrifying fight that was triggered by the fact that one of the men accidentally slept on his friend's basket. It was made of bamboo ropes and contained African hens; five of them were killed. Outside a storm raged, the wagon covers leaked and I could see some people holding a plastic bag over a sick person's head to keep him from getting wet from the rain and in these conditions, without a word of complaint, I and all the people around him watched as he closed his eyes for the last time in the obscurity of death, leaving some of us with a feeling of guilt for not being able to help.

Babies were born prematurely due to the stress on their mothers and suffocation, while in one of the other wagons an epileptic man was found dead and they had to throw his body in a rift of mountains along the railways.

Not only were most of us bored by the slowness of the train that had to cover up to four hundred miles to reach Mwene Ditu, but we were also being cooked by an oven-like tropical heat that was causing a moist stench of its own kind.

On our third day, we were all advised to register ourselves with a committee that was put in place to reunite family members who became separated during the Katangese uprising.

Just hearing the announcer say that a committee was being formed to trace family members revived my expectations to be reunited with my own. I was very hungry after three days of travel, and my lips were cracked from dehydration; I had to lick them in order to keep them moistened as I was giving my details to the committee officer. I was shocked by the number of people that were already settled in the makeshift camp of "Bena Katanga," which was a name given to every Kasaian ousted from Katanga province. This was like a whole nation piled together. Everyone came from other small towns of Shaba and we totaled around sixty-five thousand people. But in all this horde of people, my own family was nowhere to be found. The committee decided to classify me with other unaccompanied minors and then allocated us to a temporary foster family to which they provided food to cook for us while waiting for thousands more people who were still coming in to claim us. The sanitation systems were very poor. About a week after our arrival, still no one had showed up for me like some families did for other minors. I was called by the committee manager, who wished to know if I knew someone else apart from my parents. That is when I told them about my uncle Denis Tshowa who once paid us a surprised visit while we were still in Kolwezi. I told the manager that my uncle lived in Lubumbashi in a well-known urban area called "Makomeno."

But no contact with him was possible at the time, especially because he was a Kasaian, and might also have been affected by the layoff initiated by Governor Kyungu. Cellular phones and fixed phones were too rare to verify such facts. The heat was increasing and the tropical rain was incessant, soaking the sand and creating incredible erosions that were sometimes deadly. The worst, however, was yet to come. Cholera hit the camp with lightning speed and ran rampant. It was tragic to see people who had survived the gruesome attack in

Katanga now being killed like flies by this deadly disease. Scared of being contaminated, the committee team completely abandoned their charitable assistance to the displaced refugees to save their own lives. We were left completely unattended. The foster families, incapable of keeping up with the cost of feeding almost two hundred unaccompanied children, gave up. Left to ourselves, we all carried on, each one according to his or her fate for a life on the streets of Mbuji Mayi.

Mbuji Mayi means "Goat-Water" and is a small southern central town in the Democratic Republic of Congo. Its name comes from the great number of goats in the region and the city's location on the Sankuru River, making it a prime watering place. This urban town, the capital of the Kasai -Oriental province, also possesses the commercial harbor where the conflict Congolese rough diamonds are exploited and sold. Mbuji Mayi is still today the world's capital of rough diamonds; a reality hidden by the Western media in order to protect some Western vulture companies operating in the Congo.

As a street kid, my life was very similar to that of other fellows on the street. I targeted market places and asked vendors if I could sweep around their merchandise stands for a piece of leftover Fufu. Then, later on in the evening, I would collect carton boxes if the rain did not damage them and make my bed on a bamboo stand once the vendors were gone. Any windy rain would blow away my plastic bag roof and soak me like a chicken with no place to hide. I would wake up and cry sometimes while gazing into the depths of darkness, but I had no one to comfort me; there was just the falling rain to wash my tears away and its noise that drowned out the sorrowful words that I uttered as though they were at the same time accomplices with obscurity so that no one would notice me. At dawn I would start a fire to dry myself and my ragged clothes. I wrote short, positive letters that I kept in order to keep my family's spirit alive, as it was taught to us by Magistère in the subject called power of intention. I kept some of these letters for ages. Here is a sample of one of the letters that I managed to translate years back.

> "I will follow you (written by Dunn in 1994)
> Dear mom and dad, dear little sister.
>
> I am here today, taken away from you by an unfortunate destiny that has now engraved an emblem on my soul. Here in my own land I linger on the streets as a homeless kid fighting with the birds of heaven over a grain. I am writing these words so that you will one day know how much salt I drank from my tears. I will not let these swamps flood my heart, and extinguish the flame in my veins. I will go far under the rains, head bent, and feet swollen and lie next to the willows to cry out my pains, my beloved ones, my dreams, and make history and sad news as I will be once more on my feet to follow you wherever you are...
>
> Yours
> Son and brother."

Living for two years on the streets of Mbuji Mayi was an agonizing experience, a sequence of events that had almost taken my life away completely. Sometimes I would be sick for days, completely paralyzed by a strong malarial fever, lying on my carton box spread on a vendor's sale booth, lacking even an aspirin to ease the pain. In those conditions I would be awakened by a spatter of cold water thrown by a heartless vendor who wanted to use his place to exhibit his merchandise. Without a word, under the sudden shock of cold, I would walk away like a stray dog to find another resting place.

But something about me caught the attention of a man I was not even aware had been watching me and other street kids. This was

The Reality Of Our Chemical Composition and Our Spirituality

near the beginning of the neighboring Rwandan genocide that started April 6, 1994.

This man, whom I would know later as Patrick Egboyo, came up to me one day and asked why he always saw me writing and what was I writing about? My answer was straightforward and shocked him.

"I write essays for my family that I lost contact with during the uprising of Kolwezi in 1992," I answered him honestly and kindly, with the hope that he will give me something or money so that I could buy something to eat.

"This happened two years ago. Don't you know anyone here who you are related to or don't you have any pictures of your parents, or their names? Maybe we can try to make a public notice on the radio or a broadcast program," he suggested.

"I know only my uncle Denis Tshowa in Lubumbashi but it's been years, and I don't know exactly where he lives. Here in Mbuji Mayi I don't know anyone. When running from Kolwezi I had nothing but the clothes I had on."

"Can you remember anything else about your uncle?" he asked, wanting to know more.

"What I know," I said, "was that he was "cadre," a senior executive in Gecamines Lubumbashi. That's it," I replied.

He had asked me my name. "Dunn, let's make things simple. Give me all the information about your parents, sister, uncle or anyone you know and I will get the notice on TV and radio channels and then I will get back to you later."

Eagerly I gave him all possible information that I had then concerning my family and he left immediately. I was surprised that he left without giving me any food or a little money to buy something to eat. If this man could not notice how famished I was, by what means possible would he remember to do something so important for me? I thought. I did not have a fixed address; in what way would we come across each other again. He was a joker, I thought.

A whole month went by and still I had no news from any source whatsoever. Around September of 1994, a woman who was selling bread to artisanal diamond miners asked me to help her carry five gallons of water to where the diamond miners had erected their makeshift camp, a service that I accepted in exchange for food. I would go there with her almost every day until one day, as I was serving free water to the miners; and I ended up serving Patrick Egboyo who bought diamonds from the miners. He reaffirmed that he was still processing my case, which I did not trust him after almost five months of silence since our first encounter. The next day while on my water-serving duty, Patrick accosted me and told me that he had changed his mind, because the process was taking much more time than expected. He told me that he would be more than happy to register me in a street kid's placement program called "Parlement des Jeunes Educateurs pour les Droits de L'homme"(PAJEDHO)—"Parliament of Youth Educators for Human Rights." The nonprofit organization also strived to obtain free education for vulnerable children, especially street kids.

PAJEDHO had only two divisions in the whole country: the Kinshasa and the Lubumbashi branches. After weighing all his options, he made a deliberate decision to send me to the Lubumbashi branch with the hope that I might meet my uncle Denis Tshowa. I did not know then that Mr. Egboyo was the national president of PAJEDHO. During his stay in Mbuji Mayi, Mr. Egboyo spent some of his time watching and interviewing street kids, studying their needs and deciding how to set up a third branch. It was during these occasional visits that he was able to spot me writing my grief-stricken letters.

At that time tribal wars were subsiding but not yet over. On Wednesday, February 15, 1995, I was on my way back to the province from which I was deported, but this time to the capital of Lubumbashi, situated approximately one hundred-fifty miles away from my home town of Kolwezi. I was still disturbed at the prospect of returning to the same province and the people who had completely affected my life.

I had heard a lot about Lubumbashi but I had never been there, and seeing it was itself another amazing experience that words could not describe. As the second largest city in the country, it was also dubbed "la capitale du cuivre"—"the copper capital." Lubumbashi was a more active town with impressive mining features, such as the slag heap of copper residues and the chimney of the "Waka, Waka" foundry (Burn, Burn in Swahili) both of these loomed four hundred-ninety-five feet above the copper melting furnace and produced an impressive view of the town's great heritage. These monuments were built by the Belgians years before the creation of the "Union of Mines of High Katanga" (UMHK) in the 1890s.

I received shelter in one of PAJEDHO's facilities, where other children were receiving training in several skills, for example: carpentry, masonry, painting, and gardening. For most privileged children, the premises were used as free accommodation while they pursued careers other than what was offered by PAJEDHO.

Within my first two weeks, an appointment was scheduled for me with "La DGRAD de la Gécamines"—"Mining Company Income and Tax Headquarter"—of Lubumbashi in order to trace my uncle Denis Tshowa. To my great surprise, the search took only a few minutes before I learned all his details: both his employee number and whereabouts were displayed on a small computer screen. He was truly a renowned person who lectured in one of the reputable schools of the mining company called "Madini" —"minerals" in Swahili—and he was transferred to a primary school named "Zamiri" —"zeal" in Swahili—as the principal for the southern group of schools of Gécamines. A simple two minute call was made from where we were and he responded quickly. In about half an hour, there was a knock at the tax registrar's office.

"Entrez s'il vous plaît," the officer said in an authoritarian French voice —"come in please."

As the office door swung open, I stared at a big man with a curly and bushy beard. This is not my uncle, I thought; the one that I met a few years ago was a smiling bald man.

"Dunn, my son," this man exclaimed before we were even introduced.

Without a second thought, I flew into his arms, crying bitterly and uncontrollably; he was shedding tears as well. It was him after all. He had just changed the style of his hair.

The Tax registrar kindly left his office to give us space and some time alone. Thereafter, still crying, we left the office after thanking the registrar. My uncle led me to his car and drove me to his home in Makomeno City. On our way he peppered me with a thousand and one questions, while turning a deaf ear to mine; whenever I asked if he had received any news from my family, he told me to take it easy and we would talk about it when we got home. When we arrived, a click of a button on an electronic remote caused a gate engraved with a large number eighteen to swing open. I was shocked and delighted when I saw a girl walking under a mango tree while reading a book.

The girl was my sister Patricia, still limping; she was grown and looked beautiful. Seeing her there, I almost felt like jumping through the window before the car could even halt. At last, there was an end to my long search and the pain and suffering that had plagued me for nearly three years.

When the car halted, I did not lose a second, but jumped outside and ran toward her, screaming and crying: "Patricia! Patricia! Patricia!"

"Ahah, Aha, Ah," she reacted, dropping her book. "Dunn!"

As we embraced, I realized that she was sobbing. I also was crying tears of joy and I could not help asking her where our parents were:

"Patricia, arrêtes de pleurer; où sont les parents?" I asked in anticipation of celebration—"Patricia, stop crying; where are the parents?"

I could hear people murmuring around us, but after a few minutes, I realized that we were surrounded by a few strange curious faces, and I overheard one person suggesting that we should be separated immediately, while the other voice was objected to the proposal.

Patricia did not want to let me go. She was bitterly crying; I could easily feel that something was wrong. I pulled her away then put my hands on her shoulders and asked her to tell me what was wrong, was she not happy that we were finally reunited?

"Dunn, Papa et Maman sont morts, et j'ai passé toutes ces années pensant que tu l'étais aussi," she wept miserably —"Dunn, Dad and Mom are dead and I've spent all these years thinking that you were too."

Just those words were enough to knock me down. It felt like someone had kicked me hard right in the stomach, just when I was inches away from the finishing line after a long marathon. Then, right there, as I was writhing on the ground with pain, he ripped my chest open, took my heart in his hand, and squeezed out its blood like a sponge.

At the moment, I did not care how or when they had died; the words were already spoken and for the first time, I felt how powerful and deadly words can sometimes be to vulnerable souls. All my tears had been shed, my voice was gone, no word was left unspoken, and the sun stopped shining for me. For a few second my thoughts were divided: What else could I spill if not my own blood. Should I commit suicide or live for Patricia? I could not help wondering how they could simply be gone as quickly as flipping the pages of a book. They were my only parents, my mentors. How could this be possible?

My uncle who was doing all he could to calm me down, suddenly persuaded me to come with him to his room. According to African culture, and in particularly the Luba of Kasai, it is forbidden for a teenager to behave in any way that is disrespectful of his parents, uncles or aunties. As broken and inconsolable as I was, to turn down his offer would have implied rudeness, and I would have to pay for it one way or another. Putting himself in my place, he came up to me and pulled me up from the ground gently. While another flood of tears poured down my face, he and everyone around us burst in tears.

My Uncle Denis and Aunty Joanne had been married for almost forty-five years, and had eleven children. By the time all became calmer, we were all comfortable enough to communicate some short thoughts to each other. It was at that time that I wanted to converse with Patricia and get the full account of exactly what happened to our parents. Unfortunately, I was told that Patricia had left with one of our married cousins, who had offered her a place to stay, and that she would return in about a week.

"Why so soon, and without even notifying me?" I asked in surprise. This was such a special day. This was not the Patricia I knew; it was very odd that she had acted that way. If there was a place she needed to be at that time, it was with me, her brother, whom she had not seen for the past three years.

The truth was that she had left just after I arrived. I did not know where our cousin lived, or I would have walked to her place and confronted my little sister with some tough questions. I asked Uncle Denis almost every day to tell me how and when my parents passed, but he would ask me to save the conversation for the next day; soon the next day became a week. To make matters worse, I still was given no explanation why Patricia had left so suddenly on the day of our reunion day. Further, all my cousins suddenly became so busy with school that no one had time to escort me to where she was staying. I told them of every single event that I had experienced and endured from Kolwezi to the streets of Mbuji Mayi, but to me, nothing was said. Exasperated, I finally made up my mind to confront Uncle Denis to get answers and discover why they were treating me that way.

It was on Saturday, March 18, 1995 that Uncle Denis asked me to get dressed up and be ready for a ride somewhere. Intuitively, I thought we were going to see Patricia. We set out at around one p.m. After driving for about twenty minutes north of town, he had to stop somewhere, so he told me to wait in the car while he bought something. He was back in a few minutes with a huge plastic bag well wrapped and some "Fresca" drinks. He put the plastic bag in the car trunk, handed me the soft drink and we drove away.

After about twenty more minutes, we pulled into a cemetery called "Cimetière de Sapin"—"The Fir Cemetery." This cemetery was built in a garden of fir trees and was one of the most beautiful burial sites in Lubumbashi. After we parked, my uncle opened the car trunk, took out the plastic bag, and unwrapped it. Therein were lilies that in African tradition symbolize the restoration of the innocence of the soul in death. I immediately inferred the reason why we were there. Without wasting time, we walked past eleven rows of identical tomb markers all reputed to cover the remains of the secessionist fighters of the Katanga province at the time of our first independence in 1960. Just a few feet from those tombs, I caught sight of a name engraved on another:

"'En memoire de Martin Mbuyi Tshowa.' 'Né le: 18 Mars, 1939, Décédé: 16 Février, 1992.'"—"'In memory of Martin Mbuyi Tshowa.' 'Born: March 18th, 1939, Died: February 16th, 1992.'"

Next to his grave there was a second slab on which was written: "'En memoire de Julienne Mpindu Tshowa.' 'Née: le 3 Juin, 1956, Décédée: le 8 Novembre, 1992.'"—"'In memory of Julienne Mpindu Tshowa.' 'Born: June 3rd, 1956, Died: November 8th, 1992.'"

Why were they buried in Lubumbashi, and on different dates? I wondered, as another river of tears streamed down my face to wet my shirt collar. In a reverent silence, my uncle Denis knelt down and offered his homage to his younger brother and sister-in-law, then wept sorrowfully while we held hands. After five minutes of intense respect to my beloved parents, we both sat on the tombstone slabs; I could hear my uncle taking a deep breath before starting to tell me secrets that were for so long kept from me. This piece of information could have been a great asset while I was a wanderer on the streets of Mbuji Mayi.

"Dunn" he began and then proceeded to talk.

"I would like to talk to you and I want you to understand me clearly by being strong and ready to absorb the truth. Being a man, you need to handle any outside pressure that tries to destroy you, and convert that energy into a constructive force in order to build yourself. This is exactly what your parents would have told you if they happened to be living at this time to comfort you." He said the last with certainty.

I did not fully understand what he meant and the reason for his sermon until he began again:

"Martin, my brother, and your father of course, was trying to run away from some Juferi mobs who were trying to set his car on fire on that fateful day of February the 16th, 1992. As he was on his way to get you from school, his car skidded and collided with a huge mining truck. He and Julienne were severely injured and were in critical condition, while Patricia was miraculously unscathed. They were rushed to the nearest hospital, but they were both bleeding profusely and had to be transferred immediately to "Group South Hospital," the biggest hospital here in Lubumbashi. It was later that day that I was informed about the accident and was told that, due to internal hemorrhaging, Martin passed in the ambulance while being driven to the hospital. I was notified by the paramedics who read his next of kin information, and I went there to take care of Julienne who was still unconscious, and Patricia." He paused for few seconds and then went on with the story as I listened to him sorrowfully.

"We did everything we could to save Julienne. She was in a coma with a "tracheotomy" and they also put a feeding tube in her stomach to feed her. This medical procedure was called: Percutaneous endoscopic gastrostomy (PEG). Your mother was moved in and out of the ICU (Intensive Care Unit) to a medical floor for about nine months." He paused and lit up his African wooden pipe. It was the first time that I realized that he had the dangerous habit of smoking.

'During those nine months I was told by her doctors that she was not brain dead, and that her brain waves were responding positively, that the relapses were just a sign of her brain trying to resume its full function. However, she later developed pneumonia that made it hard for her to breathe with tracheotomy; she also had a bad urinary tract infection. On the eve of her death, she opened her eyes and recognized me. I was amazed at this sign of recovery and so I was severely shocked when the doctors called me to say that she had passed away at eleven p.m. on the night of Sunday, November 8, 1992, the same day of the week that Martin passed," he said, taking a few seconds to puff again on his huge pipe.

"The reason that I am here today in this cemetery telling you this is that you need to know that these two people really loved you beyond words. They wanted you personally to know that you were precious to them like any other male child that might have resulted from their union." He was trying to clear his throat.

"What do you mean uncle?" I asked, trying hard to believe my ears.

"I mean that, Martin and I are both your paternal uncles and brothers to your biological father, Mulunda Fortunat, You are our nephew. I know that it is really hard to tell you this now; your biological father and mother, Julie Mianda are still alive, and you have nine siblings."

"I still don't understand you, uncle. How come I grew up knowing them for as long as I remember? They never told me this themselves in all these years. They loved me indeed and gave me all that I needed… and Patricia?" I asked apprehensively.

"She is their only biological daughter and your cousin," he answered.

"How is that possible, uncle? I feel like I am going crazy here. I don't even know you at all, who am I to you?" I raised my voice a little, and after realizing it, I lowered it in respect for the dead. In Africa you owe the dead a silence that symbolizes respect.

"Listen to me and let me explain to you" he said comfortingly.

Right on those tombstones he gave me a long account of the past that I had never known, and this is how he narrated it to me:

It was unbelievable that I was born in 1980 in Mbuji Mayi, right where I lived as a street kid two years ago. My uncle told me that my family was very poor, to the point that the size of the family was like the weight of a stone that kept my family drowning in the abyss of poverty. I was the first boy, but the third of eleven children: two older sisters, five younger sisters and three younger brothers. Married at the age of thirteen, my mother, Julie, had my first sister when she was only fourteen years old.

Producing children was considered the primary duty of any married woman, followed by housekeeping, and farming. Like other women who bore children, she considered herself happy and one of the blessed because having given birth to so many children spared her from the fate of barren women who were treated harshly, not just by their ignorant husbands, who might themselves be sterile, but also by their own family members and entire villages who viewed them as cannibal witches who ate their children before they could even bear them.

In 1984, when I was barely four years old, my father, Mulunda Fortunat, who was then an artisanal diamond miner, made the decision that would affect my entire life —to send me to his brother, Martin Mbuyi, the uncle whom I grew up believing to be my biological father. My dad's decision was triggered by the fact that if I stayed in Mbuji Mayi, my native land, I would not be able to go to school due to the family's critical financial situation. Being the first boy and with the preference given to males, I had to be sent to my uncle Martin during one of his rare vacation visits home in order that I might get a basic education, which would have been a rare opportunity if I had happened to be a female. It was also our tribe's tradition to call our uncles fathers and their wives mothers. Within my first months in Kolwezi, I was told that I used to ask about my mother and sisters a lot. This is before my brothers were even born. However, after a year I forgot about them and because I adapted quickly, they decided to keep that secret from me until I was mature enough to be told.

Communication was something that was almost nonexistent in the country, especial between family members living in different provinces. Unless one traveled often to other provinces, encounters between distant family members might never occur, especially if transportation was expensive.

It was conceivable that I might have met my mother, siblings, or my father at the diamond diggers' camp while serving water, and they never recognized me. Uncle Denis did not even know where they were living in Mbuji Mayi. I wanted to go and tell them how much I hated them for sending me away at such an early age. I had no affection whatsoever for any of them. Uncle Martin and aunty Julienne were my parents in the true sense of the word, Patricia was my only sister, and I still considered myself an orphan.

With that concept in my head, it was easy enough to consider those who abandoned me as nonexistent and move on with my life. Patricia was taken away on my arrival day because my uncle Denis did not want me to learn the truth from her. She was told who I truly was to her two years back and it did not make any difference to her. I was still her brother, the only one she had known since she was born. After everything was revealed we were allowed to be reunited and our affection for each other as brother and sister was stronger than ever.

I was offered a scholarship by PAJEDHO's President Patrick Egboyo to continue my studies in "Law" while pursuing Latin philosophy and English as a second language. At the age of twenty-two, I had already my law degree at the University of Lubumbashi, and also was honored with a diploma as a diplomatic interpreter.

With this qualification, Mr. Egboyo thought that I could represent PAJEDHO's philosophy internationally. I was flown to Kinshasa, the Capital of the Democratic Republic of Congo, to work as PAJEDHO's liaison officer.

At that time the country was no longer ruled by Mobutu. He was ousted in 1997 by the Alliance of Democratic Forces for the Liberation of Congo (AFDL) presided over by M'zee Laurent Désiré Kabila. In just one year after taking control of the country, a second rebellion started in eastern Congo and child soldiers were again used by parties waging these wars. Most of these children were homeless kids like I had been. Having experienced life on the street, I became a strong youth rights advocate for these abused children. I was arrested and interrogated for several hours by the National Intelligence Agency (ANR) and after a lengthy deliberation I was released on with one year probation. After the assassination of Laurent Désiré Kabila in 2001, His most disputed son, Joseph Kabila, who was then the commander-in-chief of Congolese military forces, rose to the Presidency on 26 January 2001, just ten days after his father's death, becoming the world's first head of government born in the 1970s.

In August of 2002 during my probation year, I was called by Mr. Egboyo, who offered me an opportunity to represent the country and PAJEDHO in the Oxfam Conference organized under the Joint Oxfam HIV/AIDS Program (JOHAP) in Durban, KwaZulu-Natal, South Africa. For the first time I was leaving my country on a humanitarian mission though on probation; I was very excited about the offer. It took me only a couple of weeks to prepare my speech while waiting for a visa and booking my flight.

Durban is one of the most charming cities in South Africa, spreading its ribs along the Indian Ocean. It is in this province that Shaka Zulu, one of the greatest African kings of the Zulu Kingdom lived. During the conference, I exposed numerous human rights violations perpetrated by the Congolese government and Rwandan army against Congolese women and children in a war that was described by some as Africa's First World War. The conflict has involved seven nations at that time. Rather than peace and prosperity, the colossal mineral resources and strategic regional positioning of the Democratic Republic of Congo have sparked conflicts and subjected it to great poverty.

Today the eastern part of the Democratic Republic of Congo will be remembered as one of the first dangerous places in the world, where rape against women and children is used as a weapon of war to obliterate the Congolese population by Rwandan militias in the Congo. It has been the world's deadliest conflict since World War II with five to eight million people dead since 1998. It is the only place on the planet where forty-two women are raped every minute. These shocking figures would usually be more than enough to get the world's media coverage, especially if it were to threaten influential nations in some way. Yet, perhaps as a cruel irony, influential nations in the world benefit from the vast resources coming from the Democratic Republic of Congo for which people are dying over. These deciding nations treasure the most their interests rather than their values. You have probably heard of Kony 2012 film about the Ugandan's rebel and what he had done to children, but what had been done in the Congo by Rwandan soldiers under pretext of preventing genocide while perpetrating one, would be a thousand-fold barbarian acts that have caused so much suffering in this part of the world. I could document these well at the conference because some were abuses that I had suffered personally.

The Joseph Kabila Government was notified of my public exposure and a national warrant for my arrest was issued clandestinely. I was later informed that Mr. Egboyo was already behind bars with some of our executive members. Prompted by the fear of persecution or death, I decided to remain in Durban, South Africa temporarily, to allow the tension in our case to subside.

Chapter 2

The Coin Maker

In 2003, I moved to Johannesburg, one of the largest cities in South Africa, in search of better occupational opportunities. Johannesburg is the provincial capital of Gauteng, the wealthiest province in South Africa, with the largest economy of any metropolitan region in Sub-Saharan Africa. The city is one of the forty largest metropolitan areas in the world, as ranked in Wealth Report by Citi and Knight Frank. Johannesburg is also the world's largest city not situated on a river, lake, or coast. It was also known as the city of the sunrise and opportunities. As in any big city, I got lost for the first time in the shadows of its skyscrapers. There were roads built on top of each other, something that I had never seen in the country in which I was raised. Cars and pedestrians were more numerous than where I came from. I had never seen such a city before. I realized that finding a job in such an environment was not to be easy. Skills mattered more than formal professions—especially that I knew no one. The little money sent to me by my uncle Denis allowed me to rent a space in a room occupied already by almost nine guys.

It was through these fellows that I found a job guarding shoppers' cars on a parking lot outside a night club in Hillbrow, the most notorious crime area in Johannesburg. Car theft in South Africa is one of the main crimes, and costs millions of Rand (South African currency) each year to insurance companies. Outside, the freezing southern wind was blowing, which made my job pretty difficult to bear, accustomed as I was to a warmer climate. We were not allowed to leave the parking lot, even when it rained heavily, was extremely hot or freezing. Our salary consisted solely of the tips we received. Worse, we had to submit our tips to the parking management, which took a forty percent share if we managed to collect not more than eighty Rand, and left us with sixty percent. Anything more than eighty Rand, the shared percentages were reversed, eighty percent for the management versus twenty percent for the guard. In these conditions it was really hard to be self-sufficient financially. Having studied civil and criminal codes that are based on Belgian and customary law, it was difficult to be admitted to the bar in any given South African jurisdiction that follows English law in the areas of procedural law and Roman-Dutch common law. The only options I was left with were to either go to South African law school if I had money or work any job and create an education saving account.

On a rare night, while guarding cars, a male customer who used to tip me generously called me over to his car and handed me a large amount of money accompanied by a suggestion: "Hey cousin, here is five thousand Rand, it will all be yours if we can have each other for tonight," he said shamelessly. The amount offered was worth four hundred U.S. Dollars then.

"Oh!" I exclaimed, and then went on, "I bear no ill will toward gay people, but do to prostitutes," I reacted.

"What do you mean cousin?" he asked

"I am not a commodity that can be bought with money," I told him angrily, turned, and walked away.

To revenge, he reported me to the night club manager, saying that I was forcefully demanding more money, a practice that was prohibited. Being a customer he was heard first, his allegations were considered true and I was fired without being able to tell my version of the story.

Fortunately, I was unemployed for a few weeks before I was hired again at Northgate mall north of Johannesburg by a more organized car watch company. A car guard job is not easy; you have to stay on your feet all day and have to help clients unload their carts full of groceries or other heavy items and put their purchases in their trunks. The mere thought of caring after shoppers' cars made the job very humiliating and stressful because most of them were ungrateful or simply refused to recognize our presence, especially because their cars were insured and they were not that motivated to tip us. We were regarded most of the time as beggars; others called us professional beggars or hobos, among other names. Once again, I was reminded of my life on the street ten years before. I hated my government and the entire political system that was lenient to criminals and even to the politicians who were responsible for the unacknowledged 1992 Kolwezi Kasaians genocide. They were busy instead trying to hunt down a common man like me. I had so much bitterness within that I wanted to know the origin of evil in man. Who could teach a creature like a man to love so much and at the same time hate even beyond the word's essence. Who could teach a spider to weave its web and use it as a trap to catch its prey? The idea of a Loving God was too empty to fill my own emptiness. I became very depressed and needed both mental and physical comfort. I did not want to waste my time by grieving; instead it was the time for me to get up and dive into the very sea of life to find the road that would lead me to more drama, comedy and tragedy, a road that would one day take me home to my people.

I made a choice to embark on this road with a woman. Indeed, I thought that I needed a woman in my life as a companion to soothe my pain. That is when I met Beatrice Lusambo, a twenty year old Congolese foreign student at the South African Wits University. She was the type of woman who was easily attracted to the sorrowful side of men. She could not resist the charm of sadness that tinged my pale face. She found it appealing. For me she was a rare pearl; having her around made me feel as if I was experiencing an inner rebirth to a world of laughter and romance. But the danger with my euphoria in having her around me was that she interpreted it to mean that I was comfortable just being me. Because of my response to her, she soon felt that I did not need what she was bringing into my life. What had attracted her to me originally became repellent by the fact I was now happy. However, to her, my elation was self-centered. In order to dispel her misconception, I made up my mind to have her move into my little apartment on the South side of Johannesburg. Our relationship together as a non-married couple was like one of a python versus a wounded deer. There was a genuine but yet fake sweetness about the way she talked and touched me. I would sometimes sense a feeling of helplessness that I was unable to resist; before I knew it she was pregnant with my child. Though the pregnancy was not planned but one of our gestures was tinged with a fire that inflamed the depth of our desire. We could both read the meaning in the shadows of our eyes. I would call my uncle Denis from time to time, telling him about her and how we were so much in love with each other. He would laugh and advise me to legalize our union.

During the pregnancy, Beatrice opted to stay home rather than go to school. She would complain of being called the "coin girl" by the cashiers in store. Most of my tips were paid in coins, which I brought home and gave to her for groceries and other necessities. It was difficult to have those coins exchanged for notes. The cashiers, who considered counting coins an extra job and a waste of time, would ask her to stand aside and wait until all the customers with notes were served first. She found this attitude of the cashiers towards her very humiliating. I did not pay much attention to her complaints; what I wanted was to make more coins and be able to sustain her needs and those of the little one she was carrying. They were my new-found life, nature-given gifts to erase my nightmarish past.

As days went by, I noticed that she was losing weight and looking more depressed. I would ask her what was wrong, but she would not answer. However, she finally decided to open up to me by asking me a question I was not prepared to answer.

"Dunn, why have I never seen you praying for the welfare of our family and our financial prosperity?" she lashed out. As I was still pondering her question she went on: "In five months we will have a child. Will you like it when someone calls her the coin maker's little girl? Dunn, you have to start to believe in God, and ask Him for guidance to find a job for which you went to school."

"I don't believe in a God who gives people jobs, I believe that people can create the type of career or reality that they want if they focus in their inner strength," I answered her with confidence.

"Dunn, do you mean you don't believe in God? Answer me 'yes', or 'no,'" she insisted.

"No" I said

"You are very pathetic. I can see why you always fail," she angrily replied.

I was mad at her statements, which seemed obtuse to me then. I wanted to prove to her that I could do it without the back-up of the one whom she named "God." I reviewed my plans and the reason why I was in South Africa, then came up with a plan of well-defined actions: I would recreate an organization like PAJEDHO with some colleagues in Johannesburg.

We filled the registration forms and came up with a name: "Refugee Youth and Children's Aid." I would work almost sixteen hours a day trying to put things together so that we could launch the organization officially by the end of July 2004. On Saturday, July 10th, 2004, as we got all the official documents signed, and mailed our constitution to the South African Department of Social Development for approval, lightning struck me again. I came home to find my little apartment vacant. Beatrice, my bedding, clothes, sofas and even my coins safe were gone. First I thought someone had abducted Beatrice, as such events were not uncommon in Johannesburg. When I was going out to notify the police, I saw a piece of paper on the floor. I picked it up gently, only to discover that it was a kindly written farewell note:

"Cher Dunn

Je suis désolée que je doive te quitter avec ces peu des mots qui heureusement ne sont pas des injures mais des phrases sincères. Moi et ma fille ne pouvons plus rester et vivre dans une maison qui n'a pas de toiture, pas d'abeilles sur la boîte de compote, n'y a même pas d'oiseaux, pas la nature, c'est ne même pas une maison. Combien plus il serait honteux que ma fille naisse et sache que son père est un athée et gardeur de voiture?"

Beatrice."

> "*Dear Dunn*
>
> "*I am really sorry that I have to leave you with these few words that are fortunately not insults but heartfelt phrases. My daughter and I are no longer able to stay in a house that has neither roof, nor bees on the jam can, there are not even*

birds, or nature, it is not even a house. How more shameful it will be if she's born and finds out that her father is an atheist and car guard."

Beatrice"

Just as I finished reading the note, a side of me wanted to hunt her down, but the other side that was more overpowering whispered to me to let her go. Though it was hard to see her and my yet-unborn child leave, the incident itself was not as painful as those that I had already experienced. Many are those who had been on my side and then had left me without words, but as for her, at least she was kind enough to have written those few words and, just the way she put it, not insults. Also, she was still alive. I pulled myself together and contacted a male friend, Patty Kazadi, who had been given a position as a spokesperson in our newly-formed nonprofit organization and asked if he could accommodate me for a while. I ended up losing my cellular phone and replaced it with a new number just to keep myself away from people and the world.

After several days of trying hard to come up with a concrete plan of action, I made up my mind to run the organization during the day and continue as a car guard at night. Both jobs were flexible, in that I was able to postpone either of them depending on which one I was most busy with. We managed to obtain support from the Congress of South African Trade Union (COSATU) and The South African Communist Party (SACP). With the first democratic election scheduled for 2005 in the Democratic Republic of Congo, we thought that it was a better season to embark on a campaign of awareness with the Congolese diaspora in Africa concerning the many human rights violations of which most of us were victims, and the reason why we should vote for a change. It was during this campaign that I announced the publication of a book that would be highly critical of some of the most blatant assassinations and violations of human rights in my country.

On December 24th, 2004, as I was coming home from my job, I was stunned to see several police cars surrounding our home, and right in the center of those cars, my best friend's face covered in his own cold blood. Our spokesperson, Patty Kazadi, was stabbed to death in the chest. This gruesome crime came as the climax to several telephoned death threats made in the course of six months to me personally and to the organization as a whole. I gasped for air while forcing my way through to hold his motionless body, but the police would not let me do it. The death of my comrade was one of the most poignant of those moments that reminded me of the shadows and noises that I so longed to forget. The police lights were flashing all around me while my advisor lay on the wet pavement mourned by me alone among the curious crowd. Without respect, like a piece of trash, he was being picked up by forensic pathologist officers and placed in a silver plastic bag. He had been a young man full of energy, in the spring time of his life, with a dream to get married, have children and probably go back home one day after a decade of bitter struggle in exile. We shared jokes and our pain together and now in the space of a moment he was dead. I had never cried that much my all life.

I tried in vain to cover my pain with jokes whenever I was around people, but inside I once again felt wounded by life and its unbelievable deceptions. It was not about people that time, I had thought. It was the grudge that nature itself held against me. It was a fight that I needed to give up, surrender to and die. The very fact that I could cope the next day was like an answer to the plea of my sorrows expressed by the very ink of my eyes. A year later our editor at home in the Democratic Republic of Congo, the journalist Franck Kangundu, was also assassinated along with his wife. I became unsettled and moved to different locations due to fear of being assassinated too. Several more threats were made on my cellular phones and some live ammunition was also posted to me in an envelope accompanied by a threatening letter. The police were alerted to come and remove them; it was now a clear sign to them that my lifeless body could be found anytime on one of the streets of Johannesburg. My status was reported by other human rights activists to the "United Nation High Commission for Refugees" (UNHCR). While they were looking into my case, I had to survive by myself. Car guarding was the easiest job for foreign immigrants to find in South Africa. Due to the looming danger to my life, I had to move from Johannesburg to Cape Town. I did not have time to appreciate the blazing visual spectacle of this great African tourist destination. But during my stay there, I did have the opportunity to meet another beautiful girl from Nigeria in the West Africa. Her name was Cynthia and she had been spending her weekend in Kalk Bay to witness the spectacular view of the great white sharks' chase to the sea lions. She was a foreign student in mass media communication at a school in Worcester. Worcester is a town in the Western Cape Province, South Africa. It is located about seventy-five miles north-east of the capital Cape Town. Our relationship started with a simple gaze into each other's eyes that lasted a few seconds and from there it became a long distance friendship sustained by daily short message services (SMS). According to the South African Home Affairs regulations then, an asylum-seeker could only extend his permit every six months in the entry office where he first claimed his case; so in my case, I had to go back to Johannesburg again to get my asylum permit extended. Once in Johannesburg, I found that every refugee office had become packed with Zimbabweans who were then fleeing economic conditions in their country. Refugees had to sleep outside on the street for months to get their papers extended and during this time of waiting some were arrested by police and detained in Lindela, a repatriation center. In agonizing fear, I had to wait among a crowd of unknown people, not knowing who was watching me. By the time my document was extended, the pocket money that I had saved for transportation back to Cape Town was all spent. I needed a quick temporary job at night to recoup my travel fee and continue my correspondence with Cynthia.

Chapter 3

The Turning Point

Being a man bitten by a "snake" before, I was now scared to face even a lizard. I needed to get a night shift car guarding job to avoid a lot of daily face-offs with people on the car parking lot in Johannesburg. I took the initiative to meet my former employer at the mall and explain to him why I would like to work a night shift schedule, and the reason why I had once disappeared for awhile. He agreed to give me a permanent post on the night shift and right on the spot I resumed my work at the same mall where I had guarded cars before I left for Cape Town. To maintain a long distance communication with a woman I had feelings for was very challenging. Most of my workmates advised me against pursuing such a relationship, being aware of what happened between me and Beatrice, but I would not heed them. Deep inside my soul, I feared that Cynthia would one day hurt my feelings for her. But there was a kind of complicity stemming from our history as already woven by destiny that helped solidify the prospect of our future.

Having that understanding in my mind, I called her one day on my cellular phone, and let her know that she was the sun that had melted the dark clouds in my sky, that her heat had revived the ocean of my dreams and vaporized the fear and the obstacles I so longed to be rid of. I was more than sure, I said, that her rays had finally reached my heart, and indeed sparked in me a crazy desire to marry her. Right there on that parking lot I asked her to marry me.

Shocked, she hung up on me and texted later, saying that she could not believe that I would do something like that on the phone. She wanted to see me face to face and read it in my eyes and trust my words. With her wish clearly put into words, I had to improvise my journey to Cape Town. In a matter of a few days on a weekend I was back in Worcester, and there I reiterated my words. In tears she answered "yes" with a vulnerability that assured me of the depth of her flawless love for me. I caught a late train to Johannesburg that Sunday evening with a wonderful feeling that things were going to be alright. Once in Johannesburg, however, my fear of being assassinated continue to prey on my mind, as did my worries concerning my denial of God and its consequences if Cynthia ever found out that I had never believed in Him. I enjoyed being an atheist; it made me feel unique, because so many of those who believed in a supreme being called God still had among themselves different opinions about Him and the realities of the world. I did not see why I should be part of a religion group, and I did not know from which one to choose if I had changed my views. Buddhism, Christianity, Hinduism, Islam, Judaism, were ways of living of people, or cultures shaped in such a way to condition human thoughts to dogmas that would keep them in obscurity for the rest of their lives, I thought. I needed a place that was not called a "church" or "temple" where people shared ideas and were still free to object to them without being excommunicated. As I wondered where to find such a community of people, a friend approached and asked me to report to his post on a Sunday noon because he had a few issues to sort out with his families. I had to leave

The Reality Of Our Chemical Composition and Our Spirituality

home a little bit earlier, as the stores were closing at noon. Also, the fact that I was a night shift guard would make it impossible for me to make a good amount of tips.

On this particular Sunday, May 14, 2006, the weather was getting cold in Johannesburg and people were rushing to get out of the mall and go home to rest and get ready to tackle the week that had just begun. Around six p.m. I saw two women who appeared to be happy and kind by nature. Just seeing them, I instinctively felt that they would give me a good tip. But to my surprise, as I waved at them to make sure that they acknowledged my presence, one of them screamed at me,

"Hey security, where is my car?"

"What car, mom?" I asked

"You don't even know what type of car I'm driving. What kind of security are you?" she asked angrily.

"Mom, I just took over from the day shift guard. I am the night shift car guard," I said fearfully, thinking that their car had been stolen, which was often the case when customers came out and could not find their vehicle.

"What is the make of your car mom?" I asked them so that I could help them identify it.

"It is a red Fiat Uno model 2001," she replied.

"You mean that one behind the silver Audi Q7?" I pointed to the little red car.

"Yes, thanks man, we are indeed sorry, we could not see it behind this huge car," they both said with relief, while one searching into her bag for some coins to give me a tip.

"It is ok mom, I understand, I was actually watching over your car with eagle eyes," I said to motivate them to give me a good tip.

"Oh the eagle eyes man! What's your name?" they asked.

"Dunn" I said

"Dunn, we would like to tell you that someone else was watching over our little car with a much more acute sight than the one of eagles." One of the ladies said, "By the way my name is Sarah and this is Nancy."

"Oh, who is this person?" I said unknowingly.

"God," Nancy replied

I did not want preachers, for they were the very people who blinded millions of people with the teaching of a God they themselves did not know with the purpose of serving their own interests, I thought then.

Noticing that I was not reacting, one of them asked if I knew Jesus.

Once again they were mentioning a person whom they themselves did not know I thought.

"I don't believe in God or in Jesus. They may exist for you, but not for me. I don't even think they ever thought, if truly they exist, to know me. As I don't exist to them, so they do not exist to me," I replied honestly with a strained look.

After giving each other a look, the two ladies decided to ask me why I spoke like that.

I explained to them concisely what I had experienced in my life so far and why I had a strong belief that there was no God.

"How can I believe in a God who wasn't even there and did nothing to prevent all this, if of course he was there?" I screamed at the two women.

They noticed that I was getting angry and that this was a sensitive issue to my heart that I never wanted to discuss with people. They decided to leave, but promised that they would pray for a breakthrough in my life. A promise that was accompanied by something to comfort me, a huge tip, that spared me two nights of work in the cold.

Two weeks went by after my encounter with Sarah's and Nancy's promise. On May the 28th I found myself guarding cars once again on the same parking lot. I remember going early again that day because it was a Sunday and most shops had to close early. It was a little different from previous days that Sunday; it was very sunny and my skin was scotched by the sun's rays. As my eyes roved around the parking lot to inspect my area, I saw a man with an imposing frame who was holding a can of Coke. Next to him were two Asian-looking girls and a few kids. As usual, I had to greet customers in order to get their attention and make sure that I asked them if I could look after their cars. Though sometimes this act was degrading to our nature, it was at the same time a way to screen quickly in order to differentiate customers from whom we expected a tip from those who did not deserve our attention because they had no intention to give. When the man and the girls were close to where I stood, I waved at them and asked them if I could look after their car. One of the girls responded affirmatively while fishing for some coins that she wanted to offer me as a tip. Misguidedly, she was stopped by the man who at that time was shaking his head in disapproval of what she was about to do.

"Don't give him money; I would like to bless him with this Coke" he said, sounding uncivil.

I was immediately angry with his attitude, first because I presumed that the Coke in his hand was already half drunk. It was a common practice for some customers who were still antipathetic towards black or immigrant car guards to give them leftover food or drinks to humiliate them as though they were lower than a dog. Some did this with good intentions, thinking that we were hungry, but it was difficult to tell then whose intentions were discriminatory.

Nothing stopped him handing me the can of Coke fortunately it was unopened. Yet I was still angry with the man; I wanted money, not a cold drink. Coins meant a lot more to me than food or drinks; they gave me a freedom that food did not. A couple of minutes went by. I looked at the can and the man's words sprang back into my mind: "Don't give him money; I would like to bless him with this Coke"

This was a meaningful sentence to me, I thought. I needed a change in my life, a breakthrough, a type of luck that believers think are a blessing, I thought. As I gazed at the can Coke, I said to myself, "Hey, let me taste what type of blessing you got."

I popped it open and gulped it. Its freshness brought tears to my eyes, burnt already by the day's sun. I had just drunk the blessed Coke and all I needed to do was to wait for the outcome, as Nancy had mentioned, I thought, making fun of myself.

At about eight p.m. of that same evening I was still working and the sun had already set. The weather was getting cold when I saw a red Mazda pulling into the parking lot, and a young man who looked Dutch got out and walked into the mall. As the cold night wind blew hard, I stood against a wall to protect myself from its cold current. About fifteen minutes after the young man parked his car, I saw him coming out with a group of other young men who had their cars parked before his arrival. Like any typical guys, they had to have a little chat while snapping a few pictures of their cars before they parted ways. Oddly, I was particularly attracted by the quality of the cellular phones these guys were using. I approached the man who drove the red Mazda to ask him to show me his cellular phone. He was more than willing to put it right in my hands to admire its beauty. As I arched over the phone, focused on its features, the guy asked me how much I was making a day on a parking lot.

"I make a lot of money as the vice president of this Republic, but I am paid so little that there is no position currently that I can possibly imagine that offers that salary range. Not even a paid slave," I replied.

"What do you mean that you are paid?" he asked anxiously, wanting to know.

"Whatever I make I have to submit the entire amount to the management which then pays me at a certain crooked rate. For every tip I make I have only twenty percent and the eighty percent is for the management." I explained.

"Oh Crap! So how do they find out how much you are making?" he continued.

I explained to him that they have a fixed quota for each day of the week and if you do not meet the particular amount expected, you are considered a thief who probably hid the money somewhere. "They will switch me to another post where only three to seven cars will park for the whole night if I am 'lucky' enough," I told him.

The best way would be to work hard and make more so that the excess amount could be pocketed. Most customers who tipped us did not know that their money was making some people stinking rich while we were used like slaves. By the way, the whole situation is encouraged by a strict government policy that gives no room for foreign immigrants and particularly refugees to get jobs in their career orientation. The South African government upholds a system called the "Urban Refugee Policy" that forces foreigners living in metropolitan areas to look for jobs in order to pay enormous bills while having no eligible work permit. Incapable of sustaining their families, they accept any type of job in any condition to survive.

The man was so shocked about the whole situation that he handed me a R100 bill equivalent to $15 U.S and told me to hide it for myself. He also suggested that I submit whatever I had but not his R100 because Jesus gave it to me, He loves me so much and I should never forget it. He later introduced himself as Brad Eyre.

I took the money and introduced myself too and kept quiet for fear of attracting more attention from my colleagues. Most of all, I did not want to get involved in another "Jesus discussion" with him. As he left, my conscience became a little disturbed; was this effect due to the blessed Coke? I wondered.

I joked with myself about it and left work before eleven that night. It was the best day at work I had had in a long time; I wanted to enjoy it all the way through; so, I took some of the money Brad had given to me and called Cynthia in Cape Town. Later, I phoned my Uncle Denis, to whom I had not spoken for ages.

My uncle's phone rang and someone else with a teen voice picked it.

"Can I talk to Uncle Denis please?" I asked.

"Uncle, Uncle!" I heard the voice calling for him. Who else was there to call him uncle, I wondered. When he was given the phone he no longer recognized my voice; I had to introduce myself for him to know me.

"Ah! Solomon," he exclaimed, calling me after my dead grandpa, his father. Elderly people would exclaim citing their dead parent names simply to express surprise or horror. This is also used as an invocation for those who believe in their ancestral protection.

"Dunn, is it you? I have tried several times to reach you on the number you called me last time but to no avail. I did not know if I would ever talk to you again."

"Ah come on uncle, you know I cannot forget you, how is home and the country? I lost that number and got myself a new one that I did not want to give out to people like you," I said jokingly.

"Ah! Ah! Ah! Everyone is good here, and only too anxious to know how you are coping there?"

"Oh uncle, it's been too hard, I can't wait to come home if everything changes politically for me."

"Listen to me, Dunn; I have someone here who would like to talk to you."

"Who is that? Uncle, tell me," I asked, my heart beating fast.

"Your mother."

"You mean Aunty Joanne?" I asked, stunned beyond belief.

"No your biological mother and your siblings are all here with me but some are already asleep."

"No I can't talk to her uncle," I said, as tears streamed down my cheeks to mix with the sweat that had already covered my cold face. I was shivering and I could not believe that my family was there.

I was too angry to hold a conversation with her; I felt that my parents did not love me; they had abandoned me for twenty-two years as though I never even existed for them. I apologized to my Uncle that I did not mean to disrespect him. I just did not want to talk to them at all.

Before hanging up the phone, I could hear him asking me to wait for few minutes:

"Dunn, hang on there for a minute, tell me the truth."

His voice contained a combination of seriousness and frustration.

"What is it, uncle?" I replied, uncertain of what he was going to say.

"About Beatrice," he replied.

"What about her, uncle?" I asked, feeling my stomach turn over.

"We were visited by her family early this month. They told us that she was carrying your child by the time she left Johannesburg, and we needed to pay some money for a tribal fine and that we should also raise the child. Their daughter needs to go back to college and finish her studies," he reported to me.

"So what did you tell them?" I wanted to know.

"You can't anticipate and ask me that question," he retorted.

"Do you really acknowledge the child to be yours?" He continued.

"Yes, uncle, I believe that the child is mine, but the lady just disappeared and took everything that belonged to me here in Johannesburg and put me in a difficult situation, I don't even know if truly the baby was born a girl as the doctor diagnosed it based on sonogram, no uncle you should not pay them a dime. Their daughter should pay them with the money she made out of my belongings," I complained and advised him against paying any tribal fine.

"First, for your information, your child is a cute little girl who looks like you and she is almost two years. It does not matter what her mother did to you there. If you were in her shoes, you would have done the very same thing she did. Beatrice had a hell of pressure from her parents." He spoke in a voice of great sympathy.

"I got you uncle; at least she has parents, what about me? She almost killed me by doing this, so what did you tell the family?" I asked him again, anxious to know.

"Your mother said she will take care of that and raise your child because she never had a chance to raise you as her own son," he answered me.

I felt as though every inch of my skin was being slashed with a razor blade. I hung up and left the phone booth crying heavily. I could feel goose bumps all over my tiny body as my uncle's last words played back on the tape of my mind.

I had just realized my mother was a woman in pain, abused by traditions and customs. She was brought up in a society where all she could do or be good at, was to give birth: to give birth to as many children as she could. Her man did as all others would do. They did not care how these kids were supposed to be brought up. Once more, if the woman was barren or could not sustain a pregnancy, they would label her a witch or an outcast. My mother had to give birth to as many children as her womb would allow her, even to her death, to avoid that fate.

She was a mother like many others who endured so much more pain than I had. She had to release me so that I might be the one capable of looking into the depth of the abyss that traditions had dragged her into. For twenty-two years she had to put a fake smile on her face whenever she saw young men passing on the road as she tried hard to match their faces and ages with that of her first son, and she would always say to herself, "Dunn, my son, would be this height or this big at this age..." Being fragile and yet strong she would cry in silence so that no one would know that she was in pieces. She would hide the pain of long years of grief and tears behind the darkness of her skin so that no one would know she was mourning her son. I was dead to her as she was dead to me. She somehow felt so guilty but she could not change the hand of time.

With a deep sigh, I could feel my heart going out to my mother. I needed to see her, hug her, feel the warmth of her embrace, and talk to her. I needed to tell her how much I missed and loved her and I had no reason whatsoever to get so mad with her. I needed to tell her that we were both melting ice at the center of the merciless fire of customs.

When I stood to make a second phone call, the line was silent. My call time was up and it was past midnight. I took a cab and left. I sat there on the bed looking back over the events of the day and thought that, without doubt, May 28, 2006 was one of the most amazing days of my life. I needed to put the pieces of the puzzle together. I could feel that something was going on. I was being molded by people who had a direct link with me or me with them. It was an interchange of energies and their transformations from one form to another that reflected the apparent reality that I was experiencing. To be able to analyze these forms of energy and their main source, I had first to reconcile with myself and then with my mother and siblings. Three days later, I called my mother and apologized. It was the most emotional call I ever had. I had so much on the table of my heart with which I wanted to feed her mind, but the sound of her crying was enough to be felt as an answered prayer. Yes, she spoke to me how she so prayed to God day and night for this moment when she would no longer look for me in the faces of other young men. I was trying to picture what she looked like in the shadows of my mind. I could hear her calling my siblings to come and talk to me and this marked the beginning of a very long distance emotional relationship with my family. I came to understand the deepest secrets of a life where man is the biggest enemy of his own "Existence," the "God" who produced life. It took me steady hard work over the course of nine months, cross checking for true knowledge. It was too difficult and still sounded absurd to me to just believe in a form of knowledge because in my entire life I had never believed. I wanted a conviction, a proof that my human senses could grasp and that would act on my mind. With my knowledge of some laws of nature in chemistry and physics, I confronted the Bible's truth, which at first was blurred by my then shallow understanding. But by the time I looked at my life experiences through the lens of what the Bible says, I was hit by the true version of the world's reality. I understood that I, as well as everybody else, was part of a frame of circumstances defining the time of our lives at a specific place depending on our configurations that I called *"spiritual chemical composition."* The authenticity of this knowledge is established and confirmed in our everyday activities and their consequences. I drew a line between genuine and false knowledge; this said, it means the result of our activities does not depend directly on the correspondence between the correctness of our knowledge and the object to which our activities is directed because our knowledge is limited when it comes to matter's spiritual chemical combination. The Desire of man, the Devil or man's ego through the power of reproduction which is most expressed through man's activities made him claim his Creator's place. Man started worshiping himself or the work of his hands—idolatry. He thought that life was a building, he was a free builder, and his activities were the bricks that he would use to erect the wall of life higher like the Babel tower, in order to combat God and create a name for himself. It is significant that man worships the energy of his ego that he calls "the power within." Most of the teachings of secret societies are based on enhancing the expression of our inner power, which is mostly fused with our ego. These societies are called ancients because they teach a type of language that all started with Adam, and the tower of Babel was the first project in human history followed by the era of the Egyptian pharaohs. They used and still use this language to influence governments, celebrities, scientists, even religions to build their empire. Their intentions are focused on themselves through their activities which turn them all into cults of idolaters, "worshiping things or images made by man's hand." Remember that Idolatry is not a cult of Satan as a person but it is defined to be a cult of images made by man through his activities and, in this case, as activated by his ego. To understand this reality let us analyze the deep thoughts that molded my beliefs as I tried to grasp the concept of a loving God in a world of indescribable sufferings.

PART II:
OUR REALITY REDEFINED

Chapter 4

*R*eality *Redefined*

It is an obvious truth that men are endowed with a high mental and moral organization, which is, in turn, empowered by a conscientious consciousness and free will; and if these traits are used suitably, they turn into compasses that can define a time in space along with its observable facts.

However, the big question remains: how do these observable facts, which I will call "reality," influence our feelings, thoughts, and attitudes towards our fellow human being, "God" (if He truly exists), and nature in general?

What are these observable facts, or what is reality?

The topic of "reality" has been one of the most controversial in the annals of time, upon which some philosophers never agree.

Reality is the factual or perceived truth of the cause and effect of circumstances, whether they are physical, metaphorical, or abstract.

Reality is perceived truth because everyone has a unique way of comprehending facts and their causes and effects, depending on whether they consider it subjectively or objectively.

For some, every reality depends on how a particular person perceives it. It is subjective if it originates inside the person's mind (meaning it is debatable) and objective if it comes from outside the mind (non-debatable). For example: "I see an object". This means, before I even saw the object, it existed independently of my sight. It is its existence prior to my encounter with it that I will call objective reality. This object will continue to exist whether we apply a label to it or not. However, by the time I process the view of my object and decide to use a language and call it "anything" through my consciousness, and whether I find it either attractive or repulsive or if it needs to be even called a thing, this experience becomes subjective.

From the example above, we can conclude that there is only one common ground between the two realities, and this common ground is the object or substance's "existence", with all its configurations therein contained, without bringing in our mind's judgment of its shape, size, color or taste. Without the object's "existence," there will be no subjective or objective reality, and the same theory is applied to man and his existence. Man's own conscious existence enables his own reality and that of things around him.

The divergence is born when the subjective guy influenced by culture, time, space, or his origins decides to label the already existing object a "house on the hill" and bring in whole its characteristics. Someone else would have labeled it differently according to his language, experience with it or its intended usage, and called it a chapel. For example a blind man using his cane to touch it would have thought of a man-made edifice. His idea of beauty would be very different, and his opinion of it would definitely lead to a subjective reality.

Consider for a moment a world in which everything is undefined, in which there are only things with no name or label applied to them; the question remains: how do we then get to know or define them?

The answer would definitely be through "experience" with them. This experience is activated by a strong internal demand that compels us to adapt to the flow of nature. We often happen to name the purpose, which by itself might have been made available by gathering a set of substances with particular properties that fulfill our needs. This means that most of the things around us are expressed by their traits because they were made with properties that correlate with our needs. The object, or the matter itself, remains constant; what changes is its usage through our choice of a variety of properties that fulfill the demand, and in most cases, it is this demand that we happen to name.

Prior to being born, we had no conviction whatsoever about the object, its configuration, or its characteristics. A conviction is deduced effectively only when the full properties of the object of our interest become thoroughly known in correlation with meeting our needs. It is only then that a true "belief" about the object is created. However, because everyone has a unique way of experiencing objects, there could be a high probability that our convictions can be true to us and completely absurd to others; the same can be said of beliefs born from our convictions.

How do we now draw a common line?

The above example of a house on the hill exposes the main conditions that a reality should comply with in our life-view when it is perceived differently by two people.

The first condition is that a reality should be "perceivable" through one or more of our senses.

Secondly, and most importantly, it should be "truly communicated." The latter is important because it may include the first and third stages. For example, we label an object after engaging our senses with it and then processing its necessity called "essence" in correlation with our demand and our environment. Only then can we justifiably communicate its true attributes directly or indirectly to ourselves or others.

Thirdly, it should be "reflected" in our mind.

These three stages of reality are very crucial; if one stage is distorted the others will definitely be affected, and this can influence the feelings of not just one man but of the whole world in general.

It is now time to assess the causative factors of these three stages of reality in accordance with their respective degrees.

That Which Is Perceived

Most of us are familiar with the verb to perceive and we often use it in a way that is limited, as though it means "to understand."

In Latin, percipere, means *"to perceive, to grasp entirely, lay hold of,"* or *"to become aware of something through the senses."*

Our senses are the windows through which we experience all matter. To lack all the five senses brings the human mind to a complete stillness; thus a man is in a comatose state. To operate on one sense is far better than to have none. One might think that imagination, dreams, and the like can carry on without sensory aid. However, this is not the case. A person can only achieve knowledge of the invisible through what perceptible objects reveal to or inspire in him.

Having said this, if someone happens to have an extra sense, he might perceive things beyond the ordinary human's mind. This means that nothing we do ever escapes the boundaries set by our senses. Art, religion, science, technology just amplify their roles. To imagine something without the involvement of our senses is impossible.

Our description of something that is beyond our senses will be inadequate if that thing truly exists, which means that we can never grasp the full understanding of things that exist beyond our senses, and an attempt to do so will only highlight our inefficiency in relation to the ungraspable object.

A blind man can only inefficiently grasp the reality of light by either exaggerating or underestimating it. This can be the case for someone with sight impairment too. A person with what I will call gifted vision will always see more than the normal person sees. This said, it means you have to be at the exact location with everybody else with normal senses and be able to get the same reflection of the object in order to communicate its reality. Any mismatch in your senses, your reflection, or your positioning in relation to the object will be reflected through the communication of its reality to yourself or to people you relate to, thus rendering the communication irreconcilable. This seems to be an unattainable task because we are each made with a unique perspective in the way that we react to our reality, whether through perception, reflection, or communication.

Let us start with the sense of sight. This sense allows us to see matter's colors, shapes, sand volumes and differentiate objects from one another. A single impairment in our sight or a malposition can make us see things in different colors or shapes than they really are.

To a blind person, colors and shapes can be hard to describe at a distance. He perceives things through his touch or others senses. If a blind man tells you that there is no a multicolored oval balloon except for a black vacuum while there is indeed one hanging a few inches away from where he stands, that is his truth, but his truth cannot stand up to a man who has normal sight to detect objects from a distance. Thus, this will be the same scenario for other senses: lack of senses or additional senses to what we have can open up a completely different reality to us. The day an individual becomes capable of identifying what he lacks or what he has of surplus as related to the rest of the world, we will end up with a complementary reality. It will be as though a blind person who is surely aware of his inefficiency to describe objects at a distance admitting what the man of sight tells him. The man of sight should explain the colors and shape of the balloon to complement the blind man's experience. Between these two extremes there is an infinite combination of circumstances that may influence a perception and these can be where we were raised, our current location and the feeling that it provides us, or just a mood we are currently in.

A friend of mine once told me: "Dunn, the smell of a skunk is bad to everyone, which means that no one in his right mind is going to say it is a good smell because that is how his mind perceives it."

First of all, I thought he misunderstood me because for someone who lacks the sense of smell he will only see a small beautiful creature with lovely black and white fur.

I do not say that what is bad can be good to others or vice versa. What is good is undeniably good and what is bad is bad, but it is our responsibility to look beyond the act and understand why others are attracted to bad and why we are not and how we can make them see things differently without imposing our reality on them?

To answer my friend I will say:

"Instead of focusing on how bad the smell of a skunk is, it is better to ask yourself why the skunk sprays that stinking substance." We have to focus on function of behavior rather than its outcome.

To understand how and why others perceive a particular reality differently from ours will be a paramount challenge in discovering the causes of their perception so that we can redirect them to view things differently in order to achieve a paired reality that engages us in communication.

That which is Communicated

Communication is the basis of all successful interactions between living things, with language in humans as its primary substance and speech as its best known form. I take pleasure in discovering the definition of words by researching their etymology. In Latin, communication *"communicatio"* consists of two root words: com (from the Latin *"cum"* translated as "with" or "together with") and *"unio"* (Latin for "union," from which our English word union is derived). So to communicate, the Latin infinitive, *"communicare"* refers to "union with" or "union together with." Thus, the word communication means to arrive at a common understanding. Two other words come from the same root and have a direct meaning to us: community and communion. It is said even today that by engaging in communication, a commonality or true union is somehow attained. Communication requires a person with an idea to program it as a message, and send it to another who receives it; but the receiver must make sense of or interpret the message in its original form. The problem is that this does not always happen. Obstacles often interfere with decoding. Obstacles in our communication may include the fact that we have different cultures where our beliefs are enshrined by tradition and customs. Still it does not mean that people from the same culture always agree with one another even though they speak the same language. Many types of communication obstacles exist. Even animals of the same species disagree sometimes with each other due to miscommunications. A word, though correct, if spoken at the wrong time or in the wrong place can become a kind of miscommunication and cause much harm to the speaker. Few questions need to be considered when dealing with communicating our reality because there is always a logical progression to follow when communicating:

- What are the word symbols that will be used to carry out our message?
- Who is the recipient and is he capable of deciphering our message?
- Is it the right time and place?

Communication can be carried out in its different categories and among them are metaphysical communications, verbal and nonverbal communications.

Metaphysical communications are specifically those types of communication happening in our imaginations, dreams, or through revelations.

Verbal communications are speeches with theirs symbols of letters put into audible words.

Nonverbal communications such as gestures and specific postures can be used to communicate a particular message for particular reasons and people. We should not forget the arts which include drawing, music and literature. Communication is crucial because it is the core between that which we perceive and the reflection of it in our mind. Any misrepresentation of this reflection through our communication will definitely influence the message and its meaning to the receiver.

Staring at a child with a stern look can inspire fear and hate in his tender heart, a smile can arouse joy in a toddler, and a blissful shriek can inspire laughter, while to other children who endured abuse, all these behaviors might mean anything from threats to nothing. So the question is raised how well do you know your addressees? You cannot communicate the beauty of distant hillside landscaping plants to a blind man by ignoring the state that he is in.

Finally, reality is that which we can become aware of through our senses and yet be able to arrive at a common understanding by applying the power of our mind's transmutation. So let us first consider: what is the mind?

That which is Truly Reflected in Our Minds

What is reflection and what is mind?

Reflection occurs when light changes direction as a result of "bouncing off" a surface like a mirror. Light is simply a name for electromagnetic radiation, ranging from about three hundred and ninety to seven hundred and forty nanometers in wavelength, which can be detected by the eye, or stimulates our sight and making things visible to us. It will be important to note that Light is merely part of the electromagnetic spectrum, which ranges from radio waves to gamma rays. Therefore, there cannot be reflection without the electromagnetic spectrum even in the most abstract way. The electromagnetic radiation waves, as their names suggest are fluctuations of electric and magnetic fields, which can transport energy from one location to another, which implies that we can have reflection out of the visible range of electromagnetic radiation called light.

Everything that we are capable of reflecting through our mind is achieved through the form of the electromagnetic spectrum. Our senses acting like mirrors are designed to capture various forms of these electromagnetic reflections whether it is in spectrum or diffuse. Without the sense of sight a blind man through his fingers' touch can still identify an object and correctly represent its shape. The reason behind this fact is that every object emits a certain range of electromagnetic radiation that can either be visible or invisible to the human eyes, which are capable of perceiving only a certain amount of light frequencies. It was thought before that none of us generate light in the visible region of the electromagnetic spectrum because we are not brilliant objects like the stars; rather, we are illuminated objects like the earth. But having worked in an electronics company, I learned that every form of matter projects electromagnetic radiation. These forms of radiation can be discharged in an abstract way when there is friction between two components, and their reflection can be perceptible. By echo location a blind man's way can be clear and certain; by using olfactory landmarks, an ant in the desert can find its way home, because the mind is capable of analyzing the electromagnetic radiation that any of our senses captures and uses it either way it pleases us. Simple contact with an object can cause friction where by an electrical shock discharge occurs and this discharge itself is electromagnetic. Although sometimes not visible to the human eye, we can see its effect. We make our presence visibly known by reflecting light through the means of our senses to objects and people. It is only by reflection that we, as well as most of the other objects in our physical world, can be seen and understood. If the reflected energy is so essential to our senses, then the very nature of energy is a worthy topic of our reality.

The Mind is referred to as *"mens"* in Latin, which means *"applied to reason."* The mind is the place where everything that contacts us through our senses is processed into different forms of electromagnetic impulses. I will name some of these impulses to be thoughts, feelings, emotions, ideals, beliefs, characters and communication. Electromagnetic radiation is energy, energy is image and image can be perceived as tangible objects; thus is the circle of electromagnetic radiation. Talking of energy being image, we can also say that every thought in our mind is an energy that can be conceived in a form of an image and be substantiated into a tangible object.

There have been discussions regarding whether the mind exists independently of our body and senses. Let us investigate this by defining a conscious mind.

Conscious mind refers to our individual awareness of our exclusive thoughts, memories, sensations and surroundings. Our focused mind constantly shifts and changes its object of focus. For example, in one moment we may be paying attention to our child playing computer games then change our mental focus to our own childhood, and what we had to play with. After that, we may start to feel hungry and think that driving to a specific restaurant seems miles away. All of this is achieved without mental strain.

According to Freud's psychoanalytic theory of personality, the unconscious mind is a reservoir of feelings, thoughts, urges, and memories that are outside of our conscious awareness. Most of the contents of the unconscious mind are unacceptable or unpleasant, such as feelings of pain, anxiety, or conflict. According to Freud, the unconscious continues to influence our behavior and experience, even though we are unaware of these underlying influences.

To acquire a more ample understanding about our mind let us have a look at a concrete example that helped me when I reflected on it.

Air in the Balloon

A balloon is a bag designed to be inflated with air. This bag is usually made of rubber that is elastic and soft or rubber that is less elastic and harder in its uninflated form.

When the balloonist decides to inflate the balloon, he must first be aware of the nature of strain and stress.

Strain is the ratio of a balloon's inflated size to its uninflated size or how big the inflated balloon can become as compared to its uninflated size.

Stress is the force with which the rubber molecules in the balloon act on each other or the pressure of the air inside the balloon that affects its tightness.

By this illustration, we will say that an uninflated balloon has a stress of zero.

As the strain of a balloon increases, so (generally) does the stress, and vice versa. Rubber that is elastic and soft will allow high levels of strain at low stresses.

Rubber that is less elastic and harder will produce high levels of stress at low levels of strain.

When you first blow into a balloon, it leaps and a little pressure builds up before the balloon finally starts to stretch and inflate. This represents an initial increase in stress with no increase at all yet in strain.

Once the balloon begins to inflate, the curve flattens out; this is because as you continue to blow, the pressure inside the balloon remains nearly constant while the balloon gets bigger. At some point the balloon begins to tighten and you feel that it is getting harder to blow into the balloon. This is when the curve turns upward again.

The more you blow, the more effort you need to expend; also the balloon will slow its inflation and eventually stop increasing in size. If inflation continues, the balloon will get tighter but not much bigger (stress increases faster than strain). In the end, the rubber fractures, and the balloon pops.

After a balloon is stretched or inflated, but does not pop, it returns to its uninflated shape when the stress is removed. The truth is, rubber does not always go back to its exact original shape and size when it has been previously stretched. In fact, if you have ever blown up a balloon, let it set for awhile and then deflated it, you will notice that the deflated balloon is slightly bigger than it was before. It means that *the current stress and strain of a balloon depend on its configuration versus its past experiences: how big, how old the balloon is, and so on.*

Using the balloon illustration, let us see now what our mind is.

At its uninflated stage the mind is simply the brain, which is defined to be a part of the central nervous system and includes all the higher nervous centers and the spinal cord. The fact is that most organisms have a central nervous system unique to their species.

Once our central nervous system is inflated with its "vitality," which is air in the case of the balloon, we spring to attention in our embryonic stage. Alive, we begin to mature compared to our original state, but still our maturity depends upon the constituent configurations of our nervous system as invented by "the human balloonist," the environment in which we are, our past experience (the reactants that were put together to produces us) and our fracture point.

Stress, which is the pressure inside the balloon, is how each one of us reacts to our sensory world. Remember that rubber that is elastic and soft will tolerate high levels of strain at low levels of stress. This only means that we can achieve a high level of maturity with just a little exposure to the sensory world, depending on our resiliency or flexibility. The opposite occurs if the rubber is less elastic and harder; in this case high levels of stress are produced at low levels of strain. High levels of exposure to the external, sensory world can be dangerous if we are not mentally flexible enough to manage the pressure.

Thus, that which is truly reflected in our mind is how we react to the pressures of the outside world depending on our individual configurations, and these pressures influence our inner maturity. By mentioning our complete configurations we have to look at every person individually. How flexible are we when we are exposed to the molding energy radiated by everything we come across with?

We are totally different from one another as our fingerprints demonstrate and so is our composition and reaction to the outside world. One person lives in a "visual" world, another in an "auditory" world, while others function in a "kinesthetic" world of touch.

Every one of us was "chemically composed" with unique DNA. Therefore our reaction to a particular action becomes the product of our unique reflection as dictated by our genetic composition in relation to the time and space. To be able to transmute ourselves into another person's mind and embody their reality is the best form of communication, and one that all of us should strive to attain.

Unfortunately most of man's laws are based on condemnation of actions (outcomes) rather than on its configurations plus their causes and effects at the embryonic stage. An attorney is often brought in to defend respondent person for a specific crime based on what is called "causative potency factors:" how much damage did the misconduct caused and what are the contributing factors that led to this misconduct? But one thing that they cannot do is to be able to look at every single configuration this person called a criminal was composed of before he was inflated with the vitality that governs his nervous system, and the chemical experiences these configurations underwent before becoming a crime. Our failure to collect those missing historical dots that are crucial to constructing a clear picture of a crime's germination renders our justice system only partially efficient. The main role of a justice system should not just be the condemnation of criminals, but the prevention of crime at its embryonic stage.

In the case of a balloon it is only the balloonist who knows the configuration of each balloon because he is its maker. He knows its intended purpose, which I will call essence or the reason behind matter's existence, its history, how old it is and how big it can become if inflated and at what point it will burst. It will be necessary to remember that essence is the purpose behind an object, and everything that has a purpose has its life in that purpose. When a bulb stops to light up, we can say, it is dead, because it is no longer functioning according to the purpose it was created for. The same thought can be applied for a tool that gets damaged.

Now that we have seen the stages through which a reality should progress, let us see whether these stages match the reality of "the existence of a God."

But before we start, let us look at the definition of another couple of words: "Existence" and "Life" and how they relate to each other.

Existence is perhaps the most misunderstood word of all time. This misunderstanding has shaped many of our beliefs and still left us completely ignorant of its meaning. It is by trying to define objects, that humans erected huge boundaries and so altered the originally intended meaning of the object. Today, confusion in different disciplines or trends (e.g., philosophy, religion, science) has arisen from such things as definitions and our uncontrolled willingness to fit every detail of our actions into the limits of that definition.

If given an opportunity, how would you redefine every word in your language, not just by the way you perceive it, but in a fashion that will achieve "communication," or a common understanding of a specific subject? I do not imply that you should cast doubt upon everything, but we should be able to go beyond the shell of words and metamorphose ourselves into the reality of the object, about which we would like to communicate the essence or the purpose behind its life; only then will we be able to embody its full meaning and express it correctly. Someone can easily and correctly define an object that he has made or invented because he fully understands its properties and configurations, and the intended purpose of the object. We did not create existence, although we reflect it and are a part of it. How then can we attain a communicative definition of the word existence?

Existence is infinite, so we cannot assign time or space to it; with that said, there is no definition for the word "existence". Any definition of an infinite word, as found in a dictionary, will be limited within the boundaries of the context in which it is been used, thus expressing our limited knowledge, or else our struggle to better understand something beyond us. This explains the reason why ancient, as well as modern-day philosophers, had to search for a common meaning of the word, which happened to be elusive. The idea of existence as infinite is limited to those whose religion includes reincarnation or resurrection. Many people consider their existence to be finite, however, let us see what is wrong with this concept. To say that something exists, its whole configuration should be analogous to its existential nature first and so should be the elements that make up these configurations, down to their atomic shape. This means we cannot talk about the overall existence of a defined object because it will limit or exclude some properties of the word existence itself, which is much broader than the object. Instead we should define the variant in which existence is used in a particular context to describe a specific purpose of the intended object.

To understand this, let us take the example of a hammer. A hammer is a hand tool that consists of a handle with a head of metal or any heavy rigid material attached to it. It is used for striking or pounding. The inventor of the hammer needed something to increase the force with which an object could be pounded or struck. Due to the fact that his consciousness identified the need, and along with the existence of its component elements and their individual qualities combined, that knowledge made it possible for him to tap into existence that is revealed to us in forms of matter and make the hammer. Hammer is matter made essence, and it is the purpose behind this tool that triggered its life. Matter has always existed and is part of Existence. It is up to man to give new "derivative" essences to each form of matter in order to serve his needs, and it is within the limit of those needs that matter is defined. To say that the hammer exists is not false within the boundaries of its needs. But prior to the need and invention, one may say that the hammer did not exist. It is this negation that is partially true and false. It is true if the hammer is strictly considered within the boundaries of its essence, but wrong if all its material properties are inclusive, because as mentioned before, matter always existed. It was up to man to recollect these elements and readapt their primitive essences to a developed essence that fits his need. A hammer is made up of matters that always existed, though in different shapes and forms; therefore, a hammer will always exist as matter.

"There is nothing new under the sun" means man's conscious mind can only create an object in which the configurations of matter existed before its current substantiation was made possible by our needs. The essences of things are contained in their matter, so is their life, which is the purpose behind their existence. This illustration leads us to a conclusion that will open the windows of our mind to a new reality of the universe around us.

There is no way that essence can precede existence, because the essence as well as matter are all imbued in the existence that enables them all to be existent though not equal. Existence is expressed through consciousness. Without consciousness it is impossible to remain in a volitional state of mind and be able to recognize our own existence and that of objects around us. Each aspect of matter has aspects of essence (a necessity) within the infinite, and these essences can exist only if met with a conscious mind. Without a conscious mind, existence is rendered null. The fact that there are aspects of matter and their essences means that humans will never cease to discover things and allocate meaning to them.

The existence of an object cannot emanate from a non-existing configuration and so the configurations too cannot come from non-existing elements and so on, all the way to the infinite.

Even if there is impairment in the existing object that object should exist in such a way to reflect that impairment.

If every aspect of matter has its roots in existence, then everything is infinite, but where do the differences in structure, role, durability and appearance come from? And how did existence become conscious of itself in so many variants?

From this question I guessed that I had to describe the word consciousness in a communicative way. Etymologically the word consciousness comes from the Latin word "*Conscius*" which means "*having joint knowledge of*" or "*cognizant of.*" Having joint knowledge of what, however?

Consciousness is cognizant of the laws that govern the universe, their structures, and their configurations, be they chemical or physical. The nature of consciousness is to tap into the chemical and physical composition of matter in order to satisfy a need while being cautious in keeping the balance of a chain of laws that sustain them. As seen previously we cannot talk of existence without consciousness that enables it in the form of matter.

Consciousness has boundless features of existence within itself. So we cannot say when existence became conscious because it always has been.

So, existence being the infinite entails that the former incorporates everything; this means that everything therein incorporated is part of the infinite but not equal to it. It is in all, distinct from all, and greater than all. Matter existed in the consciousness of existence before even man assigned an essence or role to it, and everything that stems from matter carries consciousness within its features. Ecclesiastes 1:9-10 says: *"What has been is what will be and what has been done is what will be done and there is nothing new under the sun. Is there a thing of which it is said, "see, this is new"? It has been already in the ages before us"*. What is new to our eyes is the materialization of a derivative essence through the old which is the configuration of matter that underwent a transformation to match a new need, which is in turn a discovery to us but not to nature, and that itself is a great wisdom.

Consciousness is the most important kernel of existence but is not equal to it. It is the infinite, perfect balance that controls the universe and its laws, that is cognizant of all essences including its own and that of all matter as it is part of it, and uses it to satisfy its will and unfathomable needs. We can never talk about existence without consciousness or vice versa. Consciousness is the vital power, the spirit contained in existence.

Existence and consciousness do not exclude each other; they are called the *"infinite ones."* Both combined, they express themselves through abstract and concrete matter. Yes, there is abstract matter, and the only way we know that it exists is that there are boundless atoms that occupy the minutest visible space of our universe that can only be comprehended by a logical explanation without being proven concretely. Existence is infinite, and what is in the infinite cannot be excluded or eliminated totally. It is an obvious truth that even though a portion is taken from the infinite, it does not affect at all infinite shape, or energy. You can only change the portion that is removed, not what is left which remains infinite. The air we breathe does not affect the quantity or the pressure of the air left in the atmosphere.

Now that we have seen what existence truly is in all its magnitude and what consciousness is, it is time to hold your breath as we define the word "God" and determine whether He exists. I will exhort you to keep this view as an answer to every question coming either from a theist, an atheist, a polytheist, a monotheist or an evolutionist, all of whom unquestionably believe in their own existence.

According to the Wikipedia Free Encyclopedia the word "God" is defined in English as: *"A name given to the singular omnipotent being in theistic and deistic religions (and other belief systems) who is either the sole deity in monotheism, or a single deity in polytheism. God is most often conceived of as the supernatural creator and overseer of the universe. Theologians have ascribed a variety of attributes to the many different conceptions of God. The most common among these include omniscience, omnipotence, omnipresence, omni benevolence (perfect goodness), divine simplicity, and eternal and necessary existence. God has also been conceived as being incorporeal, a personal being, the source of all moral obligation, and the "greatest conceivable existent."* It goes on saying that *"these attributes were all supported to varying degrees by the early Jewish, Christian and Muslim theologian philosophers, including Maimonides, Augustine of Hippo, and Al-Ghazali, respectively. Many notable philosophers and intellectuals have, in contrast, developed arguments against the existence of God."* it concludes.

If we start looking into these attributes, we will definitely find that they are all ascribed to existence.

Omnipotence: unlimited power, which is the characteristic of the existence that created everything.

Omniscience: the capacity to know everything infinitely which is the true representation of existence through its consciousness.

Omnipresence: being present everywhere at the same time: it is only existence that surrounds all of us and it is everywhere through things it created and became apparent to us through nature as matter.

These above attributes can only be analogous to His being. You have probably heard theists say that He is everywhere, and what we see everywhere is existence in its multiple infinite forms. Now *"quid sit Deus"*? ("What is God") and what does that imply for our obligations as human beings?

God, the Creator of everything is *the* "Existence." He is every dot visible and invisible that links all animate and inanimate matter in order to achieve a purpose. His name is ineffable; and yet His attribute of "God" only expresses the human ideal of His divinity. What God is in Himself, is an infinite mystery not given to man to understand.

We, being one of the forms of existence, are a portion of God but not equal to Him. We were made in such a manner that we are only able to understand those forms of His representation in and around us through our consciousness, which grows through our experience, but is limited to the span of our life here on earth.

The fact that there is only one existence in multiple forms entails that there is only one God in multiple forms. These different forms are portrayed according to their respective different essences; that simply implies their reason for being, their necessity. This conclusion leads us to understand that we and our lives are a necessity; we were created for a purpose.

However, to ask if God truly does exist will be the most twisted tautology that ever haunted human beings. It is like asking does existence exist? Yes, you and I know definitely and are conscious that existence exists because we exist. That is how I found out that to deny God is to deny the most important part of who I truly am. It is not until we acknowledge that fact that we can finally find our way to self awareness.

In Genesis 1:1 it is understandable why the verse begins, *"In the beginning, God created..."* The reason is as explained in Exodus 3:14,

God said to Moses, "I AM WHO I AM. This is what you are to say to the Israelites: 'I AM has sent me to you."

John 8:58, *"Very truly I tell you," Jesus answered, "before Abraham was born, I am!"*

Revelation 1:4 John, *"To the seven churches in the province of Asia:*

> *Grace and peace to you from him who is, and who was, and who is to come, and from the seven spirits before his throne,"*

Existence, being infinite, was there, is still there, and will always be there.

But who created God or Existence?

It was previously explained that our consciousness enables our own existence and that of objects around us. Existence and consciousness, as we have seen, cannot exclude each other, so we will say God made Himself known to us through our consciousness. The fact that our consciousness also enables our volition that comes with the power of free will; this allows us to enable or disable God in us. Either choice comes with its own outcome as dictated by the laws that bound them both through our conscientious consciousness. It is conscientious because it involves the moral law awareness which is not expressed in infants. However, as infants grow older, they acquire a conscience or moral law as an supplementary tool to guide their consciousness.

The laws of universe are so consciously just that they provide us with the most accurate reaction to any form of action, whether abstract or concrete.

To understand that God is "Existence" makes it easy to explain the mystery of life and death.

How then can we define life and how it is related to existence?

Among many life definitions, just two captured my attention as the most correct and complete.

Life is a set of reactions to stimuli from matter assigned essence. This means that everything that was formed for a purpose has life. For example, a hammer has life, words have life, a car has life, and water has life.

Organic compounds and inorganic, though said not to be living matter, as long as they have essence assigned to them, which is the purpose for their being, have life. That is why in Job 38:1-41 there are places where God is said to have spoken to the sea as He was prescribing its limits, and that He commanded the morning.

You can only speak to or command something that responds. It is significant that Jesus once declared that God can make sons out of stones to worship Him. He was cognizant of the true essence of the stones not as inorganic, but simply as matter that can be given any other substantial purpose than what they have today.

But let us see why life is defined as reaction to stimuli and why should we say that a hammer reacts to stimuli?

A reaction is a response, an action born from an antecedent action, and a stimulus is the external or internal cause of the action. These can be things or events that evoke a specific functional reaction in an organ or tissue, or anything that rouses activity or energy in someone or something; a spur or incentive. Without our effort input, a hammer can never rouse to activity. So we say that it does react to stimuli.

Thus said, life is precipitated by some external or internal force. How can we determine the original causative agent? Let see what biologists say:

Our body reacts to our environment because of our nervous system. Any internal or external force that causes a response is called a stimulus. Coordinated movements of the human body do not occur by themselves. Movements are controlled by the central nervous system that is comprised of the brain, spinal column, and cranial nerves. The central nervous system gets information from the external world through sensory systems (sight, sound, touch, taste, and smell). Our body, having sensory receptors that produce electrical impulses, responds to stimuli such as changes in temperature, sound, pressure, and taste.

The basic units of the nervous system are nerve cells, or neurons. A neuron is made up of a cell body and branches called dendrites and axons. Dendrites receive messages from other neurons and send them to the cell body while axons carry messages away from the cell body.

Any message carried by a neuron is in the form of an electrical impulse.

There are three types of neurons that transport impulses: sensory, motor, and inter neurons.

- Sensory neurons receive sensory information and send impulses to the brain or spinal cord.
- Motor neurons then move impulses from the brain or spinal cord to the muscles or glands throughout our body.
- Inter neurons relay these impulses to motor neurons.

You will not be surprised to learn that the central nervous system (brain, spinal cord and cranial nerves with all their neurons made up of dendrites and axons) are made of matter, which are just configurations of Existence, and remember every configuration has its essence or the purpose that triggered its existence. So we will say that "Life" is the combination of individual living cells brought together for a much greater necessity or purpose. Every life is made up of subsidiary lives and so is every one of them on to the infinite. But life itself is limited by its purpose or its reason for being.

A perfect conscious combination of configurations of matter and their inclusive essences were caused by the Existence (God) that contains them all in order to fit His infinite will or purpose. It is the purpose or the will that stimulated our birth or shaped the type of life that we have today, and to which we are all reacting. Everything around us can *become* life in a miniature way if it can react to a stimulus to fulfill our intended purpose; so said every individual life has its intended purpose or essence that sustains it as designed by its Maker and in our instance it is Existence or God. Our purpose was causative of our actual life in its actual shape or form but not of our "existence," because our configurations, including their microscopic essences always existed and had life in different forms at their primary level. Life is not equal to existence because the latter consciously created life in its different forms.

Everything exists because it is part of the infinite conscious Existence (God) but everything is not life until it reacts to the intended original purpose of its Creator. In living categories the human life is the most developed by comparison to others due to its special purpose. We will see below why man acquired this category of life.

Having defined life, death becomes simply the failure of living up to our intended original purpose, and this explains why Adam and Eve continued to exist after eating the forbidden fruit though it was recorded in Scripture that *"the day you will eat from it you will surely die."* We cease to live a human life when we fail to carry out our intended purpose, but we go on existing in our original unused forms of matter in our different miniature life before the consciousness stimulus was applied. Today lives are designed to fulfill a purpose as the consequence of Adam and Eve's action and its curse that will be shortly analyzed.

There are many biblical passages that support the above statement: Genesis 3:19 says: *"By the sweat of your face you shall eat bread till you return to the ground for out of it you were taken, For you are dust and to dust you shall return."* This curse itself had a purpose; thus it was life or the new essence that Adam and Eve had to accomplish. Dust is an existing matter, thus it had a purpose and its own life categories; otherwise it would have been unusable for the creation of humankind. The stimulus is the vital power, the Spirit or the breath of God, that we called consciousness. When it was mixed with dust, a living conscious human being with a breath of life was made. If you notice, it is only the human being that was breathed into; the animals or plants' breath was derived from the ground and this is another type of stimulus that was induced there which is different from the human being's.

Mankind and other living thing have the same breath from God caused differently for a different purpose. And when they die, meaning they do not live up to their intended purpose, they all return to the ground from which they originally came. But the spirit within them returns to God. Whether upward or to the ground, it still goes back to its Owner, who owns the entire universe and everything in it.

Chapter 5

The Revelation of Life and Death

As we have seen above, life is the perfect conscious combination of matter configurations and their inclusive essences therein, caused by God or Existence in order to fit His original purpose. Among living forms, human life was caused in a certain different way from other forms for an even greater purpose that will lead other lives to the fulfillment of their own purposes.

Knowing that every purpose can come about only through the infinite, perfect law of reactions of stimuli which is conscious of each matter configuration and its essences, Existence (God) authoritatively substantiated each essence in accordance with His original purpose.

As to the aforesaid subject of "electromagnetic spectrum and light," the statement in Genesis 1:3: *"Let there be light and there was light"* was the word of command, the stimulus, and because everything that He commanded had its configurations in Him already, they simply appeared in the intended form to achieve the purposed essence. Everything was so perfectly executed that there was no room for mistakes. As seen previously also, light is the image, the object or matter made visible. When God reaches the turning point to create man, who was the perfect representation of His image that would reproduce other matter in accordance with God's original purpose, God changed His tactics. He does not do it authoritatively, but through consent with His profound Self, His consciousness, the spirit within Himself which is His essence *"Let us make man in our image, after our likeness."* said He. Notice here that there are two words: in our image and after our likeness.

Why does God (the Existence) try to meditate with His profound Self in order to achieve "Communication" with His spirit (Consciousness) to create man, when he did not do it while creating other things? The reason is: He understands that He should create an image of Himself; a type of being that will "reflect" his light by acquiring consciousness. Himself being Consciousness at the same time, He then decides to communicate, which means in this case to arrive at a common understanding of ideas, with His profound Self, and the remainder of the conversation is laid down in Genesis chapter 1:26-27:

> *"And God said; Let us make man in our image, after our likeness: and let them have dominion over the fish of the sea, and over the fowl of the air, and over the cattle, and over all the earth, and over every creeping thing that creeps upon the earth.*
>
> *So God created man in his own image, in the image of God He created him; male and female He created them."*

To confirm the oneness of Existence (God) and His Consciousness from the verses above, we will conclude at this stage that the result which is: *"So God created man in his own image...,"* confirms the union in diversity raised by the statement: *"Let us make man in our image..."* The narrator in the Biblical prose quoted above is identified to be identical with the addressee through the contraction of the possessive pronouns "our" and "his."

This communication style was used in this manner to reconfirm that man was the perfect reflection of God's consciousness. Most images get conceived first through our consciousness, and then are reflected through matter as light in order to carry out their essences or reason for being. So everything that man decides to do or acts on through his consciousness will reflect God's image, will and likeness, in other words, what He really is while being different from man.

"After our likeness" is a phrase that also focuses on similarity. It refers to much more derivative features of God, but the one that was ultimate then was His consciousness, vital power (stimulus). It embodied everything, such as Love, reproduction, caring, etc.

Man became a conscious being, he could consciously love, consciously create or consciously reproduce himself into something else just like God did. He was the image of the original Existence's Consciousness (God's spirit type).

It would appear to be logical and in accordance with the way the verse is stipulated that many people think that God is a male and a female. History bears testimony that the representations of God in ancients civilizations, whether in their tales, which were the same in all countries, or their prominent deities, which were everywhere portrayed as male and female. For instance in Egypt: Osiris and Isis; in Greece: Zeus and Rhea, etc.

Genders have nothing to do with God's image or His likeness but the true essences that genders carry within themselves reveal the greatest mystery of God which is reproduction or procreation, nurturing, beauty, harmony, chemistry, and so on. These two essences (male and female) bear the same chemical relation as reactants to each other as the soul does to the body. Reactants are substances which take part in a reaction and are altered by it. Note that in every biological occurrence, there is chemistry.

Reproduction is a biological process through which new descendants are produced by "their parents." This process not only occurs sexually; it can happen asexually or through duplication, as in the case of one cell dividing. However, all forms of reproduction are chemically activated, whether sexually or asexually.

In order for biological reactants which are also chemical ones to become offspring, the species involved in any reaction must undergo a rearrangement of chemical bonds, and in our case, these bonds are those found between the male and female called chromosomes. The slowest step in the bond rearrangement produces what is labeled transition state, a chemical entity that is neither reactant nor offspring, but an intermediate between the two. In biology, let us say that the spermatozoon which is a reactant meets the ovum which is another reactant, but there is no fecundity happening. These two biological reactants reached their slowest step in the bond rearrangement also called: "transitional stage." At this stage, they are neither a spermatozoon nor ovum, or fetus. This condition might be caused by many biological reasons that can be fixed.

In Chemistry however, there is a type of energy that is required to be applied on every transition state, it is called the Energy of Activation, or E_a, which I will name here to be a stimulus. If, in any case, the reactants happen to have energy lower than the stimulus, they will not pass through the transition state to become offspring. This is the time when a catalyst is applied timely to allow a greater proportion of reactants to acquire sufficient energy to pass through the transition state and become offspring. In modern medicine, the gynecologist physician will induce fertility drugs as catalysts as part of a fertility treatment.

Catalysts cannot shift the position of a chemical equilibrium—the forward and reverse reactions are both accelerated so that the equilibrium is unchanged or constant. We will see that in detail in upcoming chapters.

Thus, gender was the highlight here in a sense that we embody both of these chemical characteristics in ourselves whenever we produce anything. A man is not just a male, he engenders a female aspect inside of him and so it is for the woman that she carries the male's aspect.

At this stage of creation, if we look closer at Genesis 1:27, only one human was created so that everyone should know that for him alone the world was made. This first man had within him both genders, as seen above. That is the reason why in the next chapter of Genesis 2:21-23, there is a detailed description of how and why God (Existence) proceeded in separating that female portion from the man and made a woman. This does not mean that "the characteristics" of a woman or of a man were "completely" separated. From Adam's exclamation to God's statement, there was a reaffirmation of them still being one flesh through the union of "marriage." There is even a greater surprise about this in biology that reconfirms this reality.

Chromosomes and Sex

Chromosomes are long, fibrous masses of genes that carry heredity information that I previously named chemical bonds. They are composed of DNA and proteins and are located within the nucleus of our cells. Chromosomes determine everything from hair and eye color to sex. Your nature as male or female depends on the composition of your chromosomes or chemical bonds.

Human cells contain twenty-three pairs of chromosomes for a total of forty-six. There are twenty-two pairs of autosomes and one pair of sex chromosomes. The sex chromosomes are the X (female) chromosome and the Y (male) chromosome.

In human sexual reproduction, two distinct productive cells called gametes fuse together to form a zygote.

The male gamete, called the spermatozoon, is relatively mobile and usually has a flagellum. The female gamete, called the ovum, is immobile and relatively large in comparison to the male gamete. When the male and female gametes unite in a process previously named by chemists: transitional state, and by biologists: fertilization, in order to form offspring, they form what is called a zygote. The zygote is diploid, meaning that it contains two sets of chromosomes. It is during this stage that the transition state is reached. A zygote is neither a reactant nor an offspring; it is the intermediate stage between the reactants and the offspring.

The male gametes in humans and other mammals are heterogametic and contain one of two types of sex chromosomes. They are either X or Y. The female gametes contain only X sex chromosome and are homogametic. The sperm cell determines the sex of an individual. If a sperm cell containing an X chromosome fertilizes an egg, the resulting zygote will be XX or female. If the sperm cell contains a Y chromosome, then the resulting zygote will be XY or male. However, just by looking at the set of male chromosomes, we can see that it contains both the male and the female type, which means that females are always determined by the male. Once again, biology reasserts the original status of man, created both as male and female.

Whenever we talk about stimulus, we should have in view a formula and rule that conditions it; this is the case with all chemical formulas too. We cannot talk about a stimulus without rules. So the rules condition the stimulus in accordance with the inducer's original purpose. These laws governing the stimulus do not condition the inducer (Existence) because the latter is the one who made them perfectly and specifically to react in a way to bring about the intended offspring. But due to the infinite law of uniqueness embedded in reproduction, any matter exposed to the slightest stimulus cannot reproduce itself exactly into offspring without slight changes in its composition or shape. For example let say that H2O, which is the chemical formula for water, will remain constant if nothing is taken from or added to its composition, and if it is still kept in the same room at a constant temperature. However, when we violate one of these conditions we notice physical or chemical changes. Matter undergoes certain changes as a result of the application of Ea. Water from salt pans on the seacoast dry up, leaving behind a layer of salt; water from the oceans evaporate due to the heat and the vapors are converted into clouds of rain. The list of such changes is long.

These different changes that matter undergoes may be broadly classified into two categories: "physical" and "chemical."

Physical Change

When the shape, size or state of a substance is altered, but its chemical composition remains the same, a physical change of matter takes place. No new substance is formed. It is usually a change that is reversible. The composition of the chemical equilibrium is not shifted, which means that by reversing the process, the original substance can be obtained. A more common example is that of water again, which can be converted into a solid (ice), liquid or gas. It can be reconverted to its previous state by various methods. Yet, in all the three forms, the chemical composition of water is not altered. No new substance with new chemical properties is formed. In all these stages, the water still maintains two atoms of hydrogen and one atom of oxygen.

B.N. Dunn

Chemical Change

A change in which the composition of a substance or chemical equilibrium is altered is called as chemical change of matter. As a result, the original properties are altered and one or more new substances are formed. A typical example is when gasoline is ignited. Ignition temperature is the minimum temperature at which a material will burn or explode. It is the temperature at which a mixture of flammable vapor and air would ignite without a spark or flame. The term ignition temperature is also used to describe the temperature of a hot surface that would cause flammable vapors to ignite. Gasoline is the most common flammable liquid. The ignition temperature of gasoline ranges from five hundred and thirty Kelvin to five hundred and fifty-three Kelvin, which is between four hundred and ninety-four point thirty-three degrees Fahrenheit and five hundred and thirty-five point seventy-three degrees Fahrenheit.

There is no correlation between explosive properties and ignition temperature. Therefore, materials can have the same physical properties and similar explosive properties while having ignition temperatures that differ greatly. The ignition temperature is affected by the chemical properties of the flammable liquid. When a flammable liquid is in its liquid state, it will not ignite. It will only burn when in its gaseous state.

From these two properties of matter we learn that God (Existence) in His infinite being could never have made another God, if not only Himself or a form of Himself, and this answers the question of who created God. The fact that He consciously used some of His infinite configurations to create human being, indicates that He had to resort to some perfect, infinite laws that He was cognizant of, to condition man and the universe. Without conditions induced through the laws, there would have been no creation. These laws, once induced brought about changes in the chemical and physical composition of matter that was part of Him. In our category as human beings, matter became conscious, with a body equipped with five perfect senses capable of consciously tapping into its provided nature and be productive as well. During the creation of man it would have seemed to be against the laws of nature and, in particular the law of reproduction, to reproduce the same matter with equal physical and chemical composition without altering its original form or composition which was God's only at that time. Weighing all the evidence before us, we see that the first purpose of man and woman was blessed with the authoritative power to "consciously" induce stimulus in order to reproduce themselves. Whenever they were supposed to act under the guidance of those natural laws or stimuli, slight changes in shape, composition and even essence were supposed to occur in much more perfect ways these laws were. The differentiation of essence, life or our purpose, colors, shape and look came from this principle and through it theories such as evolution were born when Charles Darwin studied the origin of species. In the 1940s, Oswald Avery and colleagues identified DNA as the foundation of genetics. Subsequently, the publication of the structure of DNA by James Watson and Francis Crick in 1953 proved that we undergo slight chemical and physical changes as we reproduce ourselves. In millions years to come, our great children may be quite different from us. Any changes in their appearance or behavior, however, will not alter the fact that we all were made from dust which is our primary matter, and based on its combination with God's breath, the birth of a conscious human soul was made a reality. Evolution is just a conclusion based on this law of uniqueness and its effectiveness as found in DNA. There is nothing concrete that the annals of history have left us that proves that early man walked on all fours like an ape. Even if he did, that will never alter the fact that this ape-like being was conscious and created by Existence (God), from Whom all matter comes. The fact that we are matter reaffirms with force that the Conscious Infinite, which our matter is a part of, is far beyond our reach.

You may wonder now, how did things go wrong after all if we were issued from such a perfect Existence? Did God (Existence) fail?

Chapter 6

The Expresive Style of the Bible

You will have to agree that man's life being caused by a stimulus, it was supposed to be conditioned by perfect rules, and these rules are perfectly constant as long as the conscious matter it conditions navigates safely through without violating those rules. We are talking here of a man equipped with a "perfect consciousness," in which there was no room for a single mistake. Thus, violation of the rules does not make the rules imperfect or its Maker responsible for the damage. We would have thought otherwise if man did not inherit consciousness that distinguished him from other creatures but we have seen that he was given a portion of that gift that activates in him a volitional state of mind. Nevertheless, God knew that man would violate the rules, so what made Him proceed with the act of creation? The only question left that seems rational will be how in the first place did God trust man with his Consciousness? The answer is found at the end of each day of creation: "*It was good.*"

For it to be good, He had to love it unequivocally, even while knowing that the first man would not handle his inherited consciousness with care.

"*It was good*" is the Biblical causative phrase that tells us that God's love for us was stirred by Him contemplating and feeling satisfied with His creation. He was joyful. He created us with a moral responsibility for His pleasure and this feeling would stay the way it is as long as we reacted in the manner that He wanted us to, and bring joy to Him.

But what did we do if we were created so perfectly? One might state: "*if anything is wrong with us then that should be blamed on our Maker not on ourselves, because we did not create ourselves, did we?*" Is it not true that a master is liable, even for acts which he has not authorized, provided that they are so connected with acts that he has authorized? Is it not true that a master who does his work by the hand of a servant creates a risk of harm to others if the servant should prove to be negligent, or inefficient or untrustworthy?

Our conscious life was designed to genuinely worship our Creator God (Existence). This was an act that was supposed to be performed willingly during every second of our life, and being conscious, this could not have been viewed in any way as coercion, due to the fact that our consciousness activates our volitional state of mind. This was a choice that was supposed to be made on our conscious awareness of the nature of the laws of the universe governing us as subjected under our conscience. Without the awareness to act within the standards of moral laws man's conscience is dormant. Conscience is a state of reacting to what we are asked to do by moral laws in order to retain our essence. I am conscious of who I am, what I do and where I am and I have the freedom to choose anything I want at anytime and anyplace, but my conscience limits my freedom of action due to my awareness of the chemical composition that enables my essence which prompted my life. The reality is that when God deemed it necessary to activate our free will through our consciousness, He was willing to share a portion of His glory with us. The glory of procreation, the glory of being masters of our protectorate not servants as mentioned before, but masters of our destiny through our thoughts, decisions, and actions that conform with our essence. Any endeavor undertaken out of the prescribed line of our essence was to be deemed destructive. However, being creatures that act at the level of consciousness, it was up to us to maintain our essence in order to keep our life or extinguish it (death); and in either choice, God was not supposed to be responsible, but the evaluating Judge who weighs every single energy of our infinitesimal actions, their causes and effects. Lacking knowledge of what sustains our individual essence can be fatal. Hosea 4:6 says:

"My people are destroyed for lack of knowledge…"

Make no mistake: The Creator of the universe, "Existence," knows how we were made, and what the best conditions are in order to keep our reactive stimuli within their boundaries to achieve His purpose. The two choices between life and death were well defined and their consequences clearly laid out so that the first man should be aware of what he was choosing as a conscious being.

Often a choice is made between real alternatives, and followed by the corresponding action: For example, a leather pair of shoes can be chosen over a plastic pair based on the durability, but if wetness must be considered then the plastic shoes would be ideal. Now in the case of the first man, what could have triggered his choice? Before answering this question I would like to remind you that in every essence there are some auxiliary essences that also activate auxiliary lives. For example, one of the possible forms of wood is paper, the essence of paper is to be written upon, the necessity of writing is needed for communication, communication is required for education and the essence of education is personal development.

The purpose behind our life had within itself another purpose which is to overcome our forbidden impulses in order to maintain our original state. We are frequently in a state of moral conflict. How did we acquire these impulses and how did these affect our reality so powerfully?

Chapter 7

Transmutation into the Story of all Revelations

Embedded in clouds of philosophy, the story of Adam, Eve, the two trees and the Serpent sounded to me more like the legend of Rome's creation by Remus and Romulus, sons of the Roman god of war Mars and a Vestal Virgin (a virgin consecrated to Vesta, the Roman god of home) named Rhea Silvia. The twins, Romulus and Remus were abandoned to die in the desert near the Tiber River, but a she-wolf fostered them; the remainder of the story can be read in the book "Myths and Legends of Ancient Greece and Rome."

However, after a deep metamorphosis into the Eden story lines and the words used therein, I had a feeling that I was palpating the cradle of all philosophies. As I navigated through the waves of key words used in this story, I was able to grasp the reality of today's world.

Before I take you through that journey, let us look once again at the story of this garden itself as interpreted in the English Standard Version (ESV): Genesis 2:8-9, 15-25:

"8 And the Lord God planted a garden in Eden, in the east, and there he put the man whom he had formed.

9 And out of the ground the Lord God made to spring up every tree that is pleasant to the sight and good for food. The tree of life was in the midst of the garden, and the tree of the knowledge of good and evil…

15 The Lord God took the man and put him in the Garden of Eden to work it and keep it.

16 And the Lord God commanded the man, saying, "You may surely eat of every tree of the garden, 17 but of the tree of the knowledge of good and evil you shall not eat, for in the day that you eat of it you shall surely die."

18 Then the Lord God said, "It is not good that the man should be alone; I will make him a helper fit for him."

19 Now out of the ground the Lord God had formed every beast of the field and every bird of the heavens and brought them to the man to see what he would call them. And whatever the man called every living creature that was its name.

20 The man gave names to all livestock and to the birds of the heavens and to every beast of the field. But for Adam there was not found a helper fit for him.

21 So the Lord God caused a deep sleep to fall upon the man, and while he slept took one of his ribs and closed up its place with flesh.

22 And the rib that the Lord God had taken from the man he made into a woman and brought her to the man.

23 Then the man said,

'This at last is bone of my bones and flesh of my flesh; she shall be called 'woman' because she was taken out of Man.'

The Reality Of Our Chemical Composition and Our Spirituality

24 Therefore a man shall leave his father and his mother and hold fast to his wife, and they shall become one flesh.

25 And the man and his wife were both naked and were not ashamed."

In chapter two, after Adam's creation, the next thing that God did was to set a garden in the east to accommodate the man that He created; therein He brings forth every tree agreeable to the sight and good for food. I would like to shed full light on the word "Garden." You may be surprised to learn that the word "garden" refers to an enclosure, house or compound. Let us start by defining the function of an enclosure. An enclosure's purpose is to protect the occupants and everything therein from unsafe elements, while maintaining freedom within time and space. In Adam's case, this enclosure was his ability to navigate within the boundaries of his conscience in order to nurture his survival and that of nature that depended on him. Talking about protection, this implies a looming danger. What was this danger from which our first parents were protected?

Before we carry on, let us analyze the word "Eden:" This Hebrew word finds its origin in the Sumerian word "Edin," meaning plain. A plain is a place that is not highly cultivated, so it is smooth, unencumbered, clear, simple and easy. Adam was put into a protective enclosure that was easy, simple and unencumbered meaning free of obstacle. He did not need to climb mountains, or walk on thorns to satisfy his needs because everything was provided for him.

Now we are going to shift our attention to the two types of trees that are specified: One is the tree of Life with its location in the midst of the garden and the second tree is the tree of the Knowledge of Good and Evil, location not well specified because of the comma that separates the two trees. What type of trees are these? Well, we will soon find out. Keep in mind that the tree of the Knowledge of Good and Evil embodies a duality: Good and Evil.

As God took the man to care for the garden, a law is issued. This is not just any law; it is the "*Lex Naturalis*," a natural law. This is a law, the content of which is set by God being Existence, and nature being one of his forms; therefore, the law has validity everywhere. You may ask yourself why there is a law in the first place? The answer is made quite clear in verse 15: "*The Lord God took the man and put him in the Garden of Eden to work it and keep it.*"

"*To work and keep it*" are two verbs that invoke responsibility or accountability. What is responsibility and what kind was it? Responsibility is the requirement to perform and maintain your functions in routine circumstances as well as in hostile or unexpected situations. This responsibility was not just a social but a moral responsibility that turned Adam into a moral agent. A moral agent is a creature who is capable of reflecting on his situation, forming intentions about how he will act, and then carrying out that action. The word "to keep" also means to hold; to restrain from departure or removal; not to let go; to retain in one's power or possession; not to lose. Now you understand the link between the human life and the moral law. That is why it is said that with responsibility comes accountability. The Lord God was simply telling the first parents to maintain their life by following their essence (the purpose for which they were created) and never let it leave its enclosure (the law as dictated by their conscience).

Obviously, the content of this moral law was at the same time permissive and restrictive.

In verse 16 it says: "*And the Lord God commanded the man, saying, 'You may surely eat of every tree of the garden, 17 but of the tree of the knowledge of good and evil you shall not eat, for in the day that you eat of it you shall surely die'.*"

You have probably been asking yourself for ages, what type of trees are these? You probably also heard ministers suggesting that it was a sexual act.

Let us look at the role of a tree first, before we discuss an answer:

A tree is crucial when it comes to producing oxygen and reducing carbon dioxide in the atmosphere, as well as moderating ground temperatures. It also provides us with food just to name a few observations regarding its functions. Figuratively, these can be the functions of the trees that were allowed to be eaten. But what about the tree of the Knowledge of Good and Evil? What was its role? Adam has just been told that if he eats from it he will surely die. Why?

Though this tree was strange, it had in common with other trees the fact it grew and perhaps crept. Trees that creep often do that horizontally or vertically using the support of an erected pole, and they do this stealthily; we cannot see it with our eyes, we just find them grown.

This characteristic of trees should not be underestimated, as it is crucial to our story. Let us see what God does next in verse 18-19 before we continue our quest.

> *18 "Then the Lord God said, 'It is not good that the man should be alone; I will make him a helper fit for him.'*
>
> *19 Now out of the ground the Lord God had formed every beast of the field and every bird of the heavens and brought them to the man to see what he would call them. And whatever the man called every living creature that was its name."*

After the Lord God decreed the law, He then decided to create a helper fit for Adam. Upon further consideration you may find it more convenient that, after a decision is made, He then passes to an action that is explained in verse 19, and he creates beasts and birds and brings them to the man to see what he will call them. If you look closely, this action comes after an intention, so the sequence of these two verses is not random. The fact that God brought these animals to Adam to be named was so empowering. It was an affirmation of the Lord sharing His glory of creation with Adam by entrusting him to create a form of backup for himself in order to assume the same responsibility that he was given of working and keeping the garden. In fact, it was at that time that every animal was receiving its essence (role). In ancient time, the name carried the essence of the object or through the name you could easily tell the role or necessity of the object. The name was in the essence (the purpose for which its life was created) and the essence in the name. Whatever Adam had named these animals, their names could have turned into their essence. I must emphasize again that the animals were brought to Adam in order to be named *after* God stated his intention to make Adam a helper.

The word "helper" can mean so many things: assistant, extra power, partner or fellow, to name a few, but in this context it has never been used to mean a female partner. There was no need for a female because this gender was one of Adam's essences in the procreation category.

In verse 20, Adam managed to name or give essence to all animals but he just could not find a suitable assistant for his duty of working and keeping the land. He disqualified all the animals as not of the necessary quality or standard to meet that particular purpose (to be his helper). It seems now inevitable considering the fact that Adam failed to find himself a helper among the animals that God stepped in and tried something else: He caused Adam to sleep. The action is triggered by Adam's failure to find a helper for himself. The first Surgeon performed an act of incredible magnitude; He took one of Adam's ribs.

The Reality Of Our Chemical Composition and Our Spirituality

Let us explore this incredible act: the word "rib" is also used to express terms like "support," "strength," "shape," etc. For example: the ribs of an airplane support its wings and give the airplane the strength to stay aloft.

The fact that the Almighty took the rib from Adam was so representational of an act of separation of forces, Coulomb's law, or a disfigurement of the initial male configuration. By applying this technique, it was supposed to definitely change his chemical composition or weaken him. This explains why he was put to sleep, which is a state of consciousness with a decreased mental ability to react strongly to stimuli. Out of his rib, a woman was made. The female side became an essence separate from its original male counterpart.

Why would The Almighty God (Existence) do this? It is a question of the degree of pure understanding dependent on a proficient judgment that considers all the circumstances. Look carefully again; the answer is in the story line. Let us back up a bit to the point when God (Existence) created everything. He said unswervingly: "it was good;" further on the sixth day when He created man, He said it was "very good."

Before giving Adam the responsibility to name the animals for the purpose of finding a helper for himself, God did not say the same thing; he used a negative sentence to insinuate the opposite: *"It is not good that the man should be alone,"* which suggests It was good for a man to have a helper, but he did not have one yet.

"It is not good that the man should be alone" is one of those statements that are spoken after a realization that something is or is going to be wrong if left unchanged. We know this because at the time it was spoken, man was alone with no helper. What made God say this? Was it not contradictory to His earlier declarations after each day of creation: "It is good?"

As seen previously, the action that comes after God's intention to provide Adam with an assistant is to bring animals in order for him to name them and hence give them an essence (a role to play). But Adam failed to find his helper among them. The Lord God did not give up; being able to read Adam's innermost feeling, He went on and changed His method. He put the man to sleep, took the rib out to fashion the woman, and brought her to the man. Let us scrutinize Adam's reaction, which is enlightening:

23 Then the man said:

> *"This at last is bone of my bones*
> *and flesh of my flesh;*
> *she shall be called Woman,*
> *because she was taken out of Man."*

"This at last..." is a sigh that means this is the end result of a process; the final result after a series of others that were not successful.

It implies also satisfaction of the highest degree after waiting for something for a long time; this was what he was looking for, the "desire" of his heart. It was not God's but Adam's desire granted by God.

"It is not good that the man should be alone" was a statement made after projecting the danger of man being "alone." He desired something and that was to be alone. Someone may say no: "Adam desired to have a helper; he did not want to be alone." Let us see in what way he really desired to be alone.

First Adam was not ready to accept or take advantage of the first opportunity His Creator, Who knows all chemical and physical compositions of matter, had to offer him. When someone desires something, a high level of selfishness or self-interest is involved. Adam evidenced that he had nothing to do with the animals; he was interested in himself "alone" to work and keep the land. He became egocentric and thus did not consider the value or need of others (animals). And the only way to satisfy such a person is to bring on someone identical with whom he can couple himself, or identify himself. The Lord God (Existence) did not see anything wrong with granting Adam's wish. He viewed the act of making a woman as a permissive correctional measure to the first man's egocentrism. Thus, someone might say a woman (not a female) was made as a permissive correctional measure to man's ego. A woman is a mirror in which every man should look himself. What could have triggered his egocentrism will be analyzed, but let us first see the continuation of Adam reaction.

Looking himself in his mirror, he floods the woman who is his reflection with names: "bone of my bones," "flesh of my flesh," and finally calls her a "woman," which means she was taken out of man, as we confirmed before that Adam contained the female gender. There is a difference between being a female and being woman. The word female can mean any specie's sex gender that has only female gametes through which reproduction is carried out once met with the male gamete that is heterogametic. We have seen also that there are a many species that can reproduce themselves without going through this process because they possess a type of female gamete. But the word woman means taken out of man. What was taken out of man? It is definitely the reproductive aspect of man, his power of procreation. A woman being a mirror in which every man should look himself, she becomes the blueprint of man's essence. Adam now needs to look in the mirror in order to be guided, he depended on it. This convinces us that a woman is a very important part of man's progress and any attempt to degrade or discriminate against her will negatively affect man's reproduction, progress or procreation. By exposing man's attraction to his wife and the fact that whenever this happens, it is a reminder of man's efforts to satisfy his desire no matter what it takes, efforts validated through marriage. The chapter in Genesis concludes that Adam and Eve were both naked and were not ashamed. What do these two words imply?

Nakedness is a state of being exposed to all. I had an opportunity during my life as a homeless kid to witness the beginning of a fight between two young males. One was in his twenties and his opponent was a fourteen-year-old teenager.

When the younger one saw that the fight was about to break out, he backed up, telling his older opponent to give him a few seconds so that he could undress. The younger boy soon stood completely naked. The older one, intimidated by the younger boy's nakedness, panicked somewhat and was defeated by a knock out. Having studied Latin philosophy, this teenager's tactic made complete sense to me. For example, the Gauls sometimes had nude fighters among them, giving rise to the expression "nude like a Gaul." Nakedness was used as a form of psychological weapon or armor, while at the same time the person was exposed to deadly blows and severe injuries.

Adam's and Eve's nakedness only means that they were exposed or vulnerable. The word shame derives from the word "cover," or hiding. So the scriptures are saying simply that these first individuals were protected, though exposed, and they had not reason to hide. They were exposed directly to the same things they were protected from. This leaves us with a question; what could possibly be the object to which they were exposed?

In verses 16 and 17 we saw that there were not just trees in the garden with Adam and Eve were. Animals and the overpowering energy of nature in general (thunder, lighting, and rain) were among the things to which they were exposed but they were protected from them all. What then went wrong? And what was the meaning of the two trees?

Let us examine Chapter 3 of Genesis further.

The Fall

1 "Now the serpent was craftier than any other beast of the field that the Lord God had made. He said to the woman, 'Did God actually say, 'You shall not eat of any tree in the garden'?"

2 And the woman said to the serpent, "We may eat of the fruit of the trees in the garden, 3 but God said, 'You shall not eat of the fruit of the tree that is in the midst of the garden, neither shall you touch it, lest you die.'"

4 But the serpent said to the woman, 'You will not surely die.

5 For God knows that when you eat of it your eyes will be opened, and you will be like God, knowing good and evil.'

6 So when the woman saw that the tree was good for food, and that it was a delight to the eyes, and that the tree was to be desired to make one wise, she took of its fruit and ate, and she also gave some to her husband who was with her, and he ate.

7 Then the eyes of both were opened, and they knew that they were naked. And they sewed fig leaves together and made themselves loincloths.

8 And they heard the sound of the Lord God walking in the garden in the cool of the day, and the man and his wife hid themselves from the presence of the Lord God among the trees of the garden.

9 But the Lord God called to the man and said to him, 'Where are you?' 10And he said, 'I heard the sound of you in the garden, and I was afraid, because I was naked, and I hid myself.'

11 He said, "Who told you that you were naked? Have you eaten of the tree of which I commanded you not to eat?"

12 The man said, 'The woman whom you gave to be with me, she gave me fruit of the tree, and I ate.' 13 Then the Lord God said to the woman, 'What is this that you have done?' The woman said, 'the serpent deceived me, and I ate.'

14 The Lord God said to the serpent,
'Because you have done this;
cursed are you above all livestock
and above all beasts of the field;
on your belly you shall go,
and dust you shall eat
all the days of your life.

15 I will put enmity between you and the woman,
and between your offspring and her offspring;
he shall bruise your head,
and you shall bruise his heel.'

16 To the woman he said,
'I will surely multiply your pain in childbearing;
in pain you shall bring forth children.
Your desire shall be for your husband,
and he shall rule over you.'

17 And to Adam he said,
'Because you have listened to the voice of your wife
and have eaten of the tree
of which I commanded you,
'You shall not eat of it,'
cursed is the ground because of you;
in pain you shall eat of it all the days of your life;

18 thorns and thistles it shall bring forth for you;
and you shall eat the plants of the field.

19 By the sweat of your face
you shall eat bread,

till you return to the ground,
for out of it you were taken;
for you are dust,
and to dust you shall return.'

20 *The man called his wife's name Eve, because she was the mother of all living.*

21 *And the Lord God made for Adam and for his wife garments of skins and clothed them.*

22 *Then the Lord God said, "Behold, the man has become like one of us in knowing good and evil. Now, lest he reach out his hand and take also of the tree of life and eat, and live forever—"*

23 *therefore the Lord God sent him out from the Garden of Eden to work the ground from which he was taken.*

24 *He drove out the man, and at the east of the Garden of Eden he placed the cherubim and a flaming sword that turned every way to guard the way to the tree of life."*

Chapter 3 of the book of Genesis introduces us to a personality previously unfamiliar in our story. We all know that God created beasts but none of them was mentioned before by its name. The serpent is the first to be named and is described to be craftier than any other beast of the field. What does this description entail concerning the serpent's essence? Remember the term: its essence is in its name or vice-versa. A serpent is a reptile that creeps or moves stealthily and cautiously. This movement of a serpent is very important in our story because it reminds us of the creeping way of some trees, as described earlier. In proverbs 30: 18-19 the serpent way on rock is among the three things that Solomon did not understand, but they just are.

However, this was not the serpent's form of today when Eve met him. What we know is that it was speaking, walking, which are very common features of a human being. Thus, a human is called a serpent if is a sly or treacherous person, especially one who exploits a position of trust in order to betray it. Here we find again a duality (man, beast)

"Craftiness" or "cunning" are also words that engender two characters (a duality): "a virtue" and "a vice" put together like the Knowledge of Good and Evil. They are referred to as a virtue when they mean delicately pleasing, cute, skillful, intelligent, executed with or exhibiting ingenuity. They are referred to as a vice when they mean: marked by or given to artful subtlety and deceptiveness. Before we put our picture together let us see what the serpent does. The serpent speaks: *"Did God actually say, 'You shall not eat of any tree in the garden?'"*

This is not just any question. For me as a Latin scholar this is what we call "Ciceronian style," fully detailed in "Catalina orations". This is a short question that does not fall in place and is aimed at engaging your interlocutor.

An engaging question has the characteristic of compelling our conversational partner to go beyond gathering facts and make constructive decisions in relation to the problem. It makes them reflect and evaluate with a sense of curiosity and bewilderment and finally forge the answer if they do not have it. Due to the nature of the question, Eve happened to counterfeit the truth, and gave twist to the context of the original commandment: The tree of the Knowledge of Good and Evil takes the place of the tree of Life and she adds that they were prohibited to touch its fruit lest they die. Seeing by her response that he has caught her off guard, the serpent uses his craftiness, and prepares a venom of descriptive words that will be used as a second stimulus to destroy Eve's original essence: *"For God knows that when you eat of it your eyes will be opened, and you will be like God, knowing good and evil."* When the woman understood this, something happened inside her that acted on her reason. The Bible describes it this way: *"So when the woman saw that the tree was good for food, and that it was a delight to the eyes, and that the tree was to be desired to make one wise, she took of its fruit and ate, and she also gave some to her husband who was with her, and he ate."*

It is not a random procedural tactic that the serpent used in order to derail the woman. He knew that she was the blueprint (the mirror) that Adam would refer himself to before doing anything, and making her fall would make it easy to overturn the man who depended on her.

We have now reached now the point of a great revelation: in order to understand the meaning of the tree of Life and the tree of the Knowledge of Good and Evil, we have to look at their essences. The fact is that there were many other trees in the Garden of Eden (enclosure), none of them was highlighted as the two trees, and this was due to the purpose behind them. To start, let us look at the word "knowledge."

Knowledge is the fact or condition of being familiar with something through experience with or a link to it, the fact of being aware of something, its chemical and physical configuration, and a range of information of how it is created. Thus said, the Knowledge of Good and Evil is the Supreme Knowledge because it is cognizant of all chemical and physical configurations of all matter and what destroys them if need be. It is capable of tapping into matter to consciously create and destroy anything depending on the will of its owner while still balancing with justice the laws of the universe. This type of knowledge is the exclusive purview of God. In the Garden of Eden (the enclosure) God allowed man to eat all types of trees, inclusive of the tree of Life; for the latter was man's essence. He did not allow him to eat from the tree of the Knowledge of Good and Evil because He alone is God. The act of interfering with such a law can induce a type of stimulus that alters our essence, and thus disrupt our life. To be a creator, we must first have the scheme of the object we want to create, whose essence will reflect the purpose for which it was made. Once this scheme is reinforced by a will to materialize it, then we must have full knowledge of its chemical and physical configurations in relation to time and its location in space. As we navigate through the laws of the scheme, pure perfection is required to achieve the desired result. Speaking of perfection you must avoid errors, but it is impossible avoid errors without knowing them first. The saying, *"The better way to avoid errors is to make them"* is accurate in the sense that we learn from our errors so that we do not repeat them. If all errors related to the creation of something are known, then we achieve the knowledge of Good and Evil, and with it nothing will stop us from achieving the object of our creation. The serpent did not "totally" lie when telling Eve that she and Adam would be like God in knowing Good and Evil if they ate from the tree. Where he "completely" lied was in telling them that they would not die. On the other hand, the purpose behind the other tree is Life, which was attributed to man. Life was the reason for which man was created, the purpose behind his being as shown previously. Now let us shift our attention to the words: "Eat from." We all need to eat to survive. Food supplies us with energy necessary for carrying out basic physiological processes that keep us alive and allow us to carry out our daily activities. However, God was not talking about the type of food that sustains our physical bodies. Instead, it was an instructional statement: *"I have created in you everything that you are,* make use of it as you want, provided that you keep yourselves within the enclosure, but do not attempt to get out of it and try to be me because this attitude will alter what I made you to be." These instructions were allegorically represented as fruits. As we all know, there is always a link between fruits and a tree, so are instructions to the law. Thus, the serpent was telling Eve to violate the instructions of the law given by God under the allegation that these were purposely delivered to keep them from being like God.

The Unconditional Love Myth

It has been settled by a series of sermons in many Christian churches that God trusted man though being aware of the outcome of his disobedience, to show "His unconditional love." Churches have gone as far as to explain that the tree of life and the tree of the knowledge of Good and Evil were a set of two separate traits that reflected God's infinite love. There would not have been the need of reflecting this side of unconditional love if man was just too perfect in his deed, they say.

What is unconditional Love?

It is unfortunate that most of us have no idea what unconditional love really is. In my early youth, I observed that people were willing to show me love and accommodate me as their son when I was able to bring something to contribute to their daily food rations, but whenever I encountered financial issues or my day went wrong, I had no rights to enjoy their kindness—when I had little money, *"that was good"* —people "loved" me and treated me as their son. They smiled at me and spoke with kindness. As I mentioned previously, I also saw that when I was broke, *"that was bad,"* and all those signs of "love" instantly vanished. On the other hand I also observed the love of a parent towards his child that seems to transcend beyond physical bonds.

I understood by this consistent experience that love was an emotion that was conditional. What does this mean? It simply means that love, being an emotion can only be initiated by something that makes us feel good, and the contrast brings hate or discontentment. Hate and love are both emotions but are caused differently. Can we talk about love that is unconditional? And if so, what could be wrong with this type of love? Love from the Latin word *"amàre"* means strong affection arising from personal and purely emotional ties. From a man's perspective, these emotional ties can be triggered by moral responsibility, kinship, sexual desire and common goals, to name a few.

I am going to decipher the term "unconditional love" from the perspective of what Love truly is. To start, let us see what the adjective "unconditional" means. As you probably know, unconditional is the opposite of conditional, so in order to define the word unconditional, let us look first at what does "conditional" mean.

"Conditional" depends on a condition or conditions or anything that is allowed on certain terms. It can also mean anything made or granted according to certain defined requirements, something the existence of which is influenced by another existing entity. Therefore, if the manifestation of love relates to any particular requirement, it is not by definition unconditional, and so it is the same when its existence depends on another existing entity. Unconditional and conditional can be used nowadays as adjectives to determine defined requirements that need to be met in order to get access to a "specific" privilege. It is only within the limit of these conventional requirements that someone can label one's access to a privilege conditional or unconditional.

We usually use the word love to refer to everything from passion, and preferences to gratitude, feeling and commitment: *"I will always love you"* said much often in marriage. So, if the manifestation of love relates to any particular condition (willingness, time, circumstance, life, influence or requirement), it is not by definition unconditional.

The love of parents for their children and vice versa is not unconditional. It depends on the circumstance of being related by birth or adoption. There cannot be a grant without a will to do so, and the fact that we want or are willing to offer anything, the object offered becomes conditional on our will or want.

Not even the love of our friends is unconditional: It depends on shared benefits, mutual support, communication, and all the other ingredients that make our friendship meaningful.

Sexual love is not unconditional: it depends on the sexual attraction between the participants. The list of conditional emotions and behavior is extensive.

For something to be unconditional it should have a Supreme power that makes it exist by itself from "all angles." It should have its own life. So said, because man does not have the ultimate power to exist "by himself," we will conclude that nothing unconditional can come out of the mortal man if not only within the guidelines of his own defined terms and conditions. Anything that emanates from man and depends on his life is ephemeral; once life stops, it vanishes too. Unconditional is eternal, unchanging, steady, constant, untradeable and indefinable and there is only one entity that represents these attributes: God; and this is what defines God as being Love, true Love that which is supreme and is not associated with us at all. Anything that is related to us as a consequence of God being Love (unconditional) can only be a form of it. Due to the fact that any form can be actuated on to bring about derivatives, we will say that unconditional love, which is God by its definition becomes conditional to us through the purpose for which we were created. Without us human beings in the picture,

God (Love) remains God (Love). You may wonder if an object's form is the actual object. Definitely, an object's form cannot entirely be the actual object, but it can embody its physical properties and function like the authentic object, all depends on the essence allocated to it.

Getting back to unconditional love, it does not come and go, it is just there. Therefore there is unconditional love within the entire universe at all times, that connects everything, and that is God, and we reflect His form or likeness. By reflecting God, we also reflect His nature. Remember a reflection is the image or a form of the original object that can be materialized into another tangible object that is the form of the original. This leads us to an additional conclusion that we can only reflect the unconditional Love through its various forms, but not possess it because we are too undependable to contain God. We cannot own or possess God.

So said, unconditional Love exists between God and His relationship with humans in a sense that Good and Evil can all come from God (Existence) depending on man's activation forces on the laws of nature. However, God still provides an equal opportunity to anyone who genuinely wants access to Him.

It is not that God loves everyone (evildoers and righteous) unconditionally. Man was conditioned by the laws that sustain His purpose and the latter sustains his life. Hence human love is reflected as an emotional reaction, and every emotion is prompted by something, and everything that is prompted by something cannot be unconditional because its existence depends on its causative agent. Once a causative factor is ruled out, so will be its effects. Even though you feel like loving with no strings attached, remember that with emotions the aftermath feelings can actually be at the same time the causes that motivated us to act in a certain way after reminiscing how it felt in past after having similar experiences. We have seen men capitalizing on good moral deeds just because the response that they receive afterward is totally priceless and uplifting. Love cannot be given, it can only be perceived as a form of energy. Matthew 22:39 says: *"And the second is like it: 'Love others as you love yourself'"* only means you have to perceive others as God's image as you are. God being Love and you being formed in His image, entails that you are that reflection of Love, and so are others. Some Christians will argue that Jesus taught us to love our enemies unconditionally even when they cause us harm. To be emotionally impelled to love someone who does us harm does not mean we should tolerate his evil deeds. The type of love that we should express to our enemy is the one that is triggered by a desire to see our enemy genuinely change his evil ways and be again a good person while still alive. When Jesus made the above statement, He was fully aware of the nature of men when it comes to vengeance: *"Eye for an eye, tooth for tooth"* is what kindles in the spirit of man when offended. This vengeful attitude can be the primary cause of extreme wickedness in the world. The reason is that when man wants to harm his fellow human being or enemy, he owes it to himself to execute that injury to extreme so that any vengeance that might come from his enemy will not be dreaded in any way even if his victim survives. It is from this philosophy that Machiavelli inspired himself.

It is when this vengeful thought conquers our mind that our love should strive to be expressed in the form of the message to our enemy that we are not willing to commit vengeance. This is for the sole purpose of inspiring him to change his evil ways. It is this type of Love that should be expressed by us when an evildoer repents, because without it true forgiveness cannot take place; instead it will be a vengeance-driven reaction. The Bible definition of Love is bi-dimensional: Firstly, because God is Love (Unconditional and untradeable) and secondly, because the love that exudes from a moral perspective (conditional) comes forth from within a perfect moral standard. It is impossible for God (Existence) to love outside His moral nature with which He conditioned man. So said, God cannot love without those conditions being met under the form of natural laws. Talking of natural laws, we must also mention about natural justice.

There can be no validity in the idea that a Morally-Perfect God can love a person unconditionally because this thought itself annihilates the eminence of repentance and forgiveness, which are both requirements set by God. This truth about love is the foundation for asserting all human rights and personal freedoms. There must always be conditions to love in order to provide liberty and freedom from wrong. If one loves justice then one hates injustice. If one loves independence, then one despises the evils of unjust enslavement. God being Love has proven to us sufficiently that He has consigned time during which we should understand that He still hopes that at some time we will realize that we have wronged Him and that He never intended to avenge.

The Serpent

But who was this serpent and why does it play the role of a deceiver? This serpent, as described in the Bible, is not an ordinary serpent as we know today. As described previously, it talked, walked and of course crept because that is what the word "serpent" means. Talking is to communicate or express ideas, messages in words to oneself or to others. There have been many misconceptions when it comes to the art of communicating ideas through words. The truth is that every conscious man can never talk to someone else without talking to himself first, and whenever this rule is violated it renders man a fool.

Proverbs 18:2 says: "*A fool takes no pleasure in understanding, but only in expressing his opinion.*"

By talking to himself, a man becomes conscious of his thoughts and thus acquires understanding before expressing them. It is between our consciousness and our volitional state of mind (free will) that the cradle of every man's words (communication) resides. However, it is between our volitional state of mind and our conscience (what we are asked to do by the moral law in order to keep our essence) that a desire is born. We will say conclusively that a desire is the chosen course of action with regard to or regardless of our conscience. When God created the first man, the latter was endowed with a desire that was to be guided by his conscience in order to achieve God's will while maintaining his essence. In his share of the creation's glory, man was allowed to implement his desire as long as it did not violate the boundaries set by God. By comparison, the serpent had two attributes with a dual meaning and these are the same duality portrayed in the word "cunning" or "crafty." So we will say that serpent (desire) in man was talking of God's supremacy. The desire did not go straight for fear of being discovered; instead, it took the nature of a serpent, which zigzags (creeps), and bit him when he was more vulnerable as two separate genders. When Adam desired to have a helper, it was granted to him because his desired wish did not conflict with God's laws. It did not interfere with God's supremacy.

Let us look at the story again just a few moments beforehand; something amazing had happened prior to the woman eating from the tree and sharing it with her husband: *"the tree was to be desired to make one wise."* It was only then that she took its fruits and ate. To conclude, the desire was the embodiment of everything above mentioned. A desire was the talking serpent questioning the supremacy of God that was represented by the tree of the Knowledge of Good and Evil, thus challenging the moral law decreed by God (Existence). It was the desire that activated the second stimulus that compelled Adam to underestimate the animals by not finding a helper among them, and finally pushed him to request that the female part of him be separate. This means that it is all Adam's fault because the woman was originally part of him. It was here that our ego was exposed. As we know, every desire needs a choice in order to exist; in other words, it walks or wanders between choices. Like and dislike, attachment, aversion, greed and hatred are the primary activities of the ego. In reality, the ego depends on desire. The more we go on expressing our desire, the more the ego seems to be hidden from us, but when our desire is satisfied, our ego, which appeared dormant during the execution of our desire, becomes exposed, and we then become ashamed by our action. The ego is differently expressed in children than in adults. The difference is based on the consciousness of our conscience (the moral law). A child is not conscious of the moral law; this lack of awareness of the moral law renders his ego naïve or innocent. We adults are conscious and this attitude enables our aptitude to control our ego, thus rendering it less expressive. Matthew 18:3:

> And he said: "I tell you the truth, unless you change and become like little children, you will never enter the kingdom of heaven..."

Failure to do this is called: egotism or pride.

We definitely have had times in our life when we have said that we were faced with a strong desire to do something, and nobody could stop us from achieving it. Not even death could stop us, because our strong desire blurred our reason. We need to point out that our conscious reason, which protects our inner self, ceases to act as a protective safety valve when our desire becomes stronger than reason. Therefore, our nudity becomes apparent to ourselves and we become ashamed after fulfilling our desire. Have you ever asked yourself why a good man commits a crime? If you have enough courage to delve into the emotions and passions that he had just before committing these erroneous acts, you have obviously found the changing nature of the serpent that crept into his inner self and silenced his reason to make him completely bare to his shame. But this will be seen in the next chapter. However, what can be interpreted from the phrase: *"their eyes became opened just as they ate the fruit?"* It confirms that the serpent of desire was right, a huge transition took place, they realized that they were indeed naked or exposed to forces of nature that were much bigger in their glory than theirs. Nature became overpowering and frightening; it turned out to be so immense that they felt they were too tiny to control it. In a state of panic, they covered themselves with fig leaves to feel protected. This self-protection, however, was not enough to shield them from the voice of their Maker, which was far greater than nature itself. No longer able to contain themselves, they hid from Him. The fig leaves were their way of trying to cover or atone for their own sin.

Chapter 8

The Power of the Eden's Curse on us

When confronted by his Maker, Adam did not recite the "*mea maxima culpa*" (It is my grievous mistake) to express humility or repentance. Instead, he blamed it on his wife Eve. When questioned, she, in her accused the serpent of misguidance. It is not a random act that God started by asking Adam. He knew that it was his desire that unleashed the trouble, but Adam denied wrong doing. God turned to the woman hoping that her, being Adam's mirror, she would be contrite and repent, but she too, being the product of man's desire accuses the serpent (the desire). It becomes a vicious circle. Their attitude is that of people who do not want to accept blame and be accountable for it. This attitude is reflected up to today as we keep blaming our shortcomings on the serpent "Satan."

If you noticed, God did not ask the serpent, instead, He directly imposed a curse on it. He knew that it was the one questioning His laws and supremacy:

> "Because you have done this,
> cursed are you above all livestock

and above all beasts of the field;
on your belly you shall go,
and dust you shall eat
all the days of your life.

15 I will put enmity between you and the woman,
and between your offspring and her offspring;
he shall bruise your head,
and you shall bruise his heel."

There is a great similarity in each curse and decoding their messages is paramount to understanding our reality: Desire, being the serpent, is the great longing within us, it is that passion that cannot be stopped by anyone, and which only death can extinguish. It is above everything, including every beast of the field that is guided by instinct that cannot exceed man's desire. The serpent was that form of desire in Adam and Eve that acted like a switch between their subordination to and oneness with God. It is within this limit as a switch that it was designed to be controlled. But the first man misused it and he was now willing to be God himself (*"you will be like God"*). This incredible allowance of being in God's likeness shows us how much further the Almighty went in loving a man made of dust.

To walk on the belly entails a sense of much pain and inability to stand. This means it will be difficult for our desires to stand or to be achieved; they are for the rest of our lives cursed to creep. And even if our ego thinks that it is still standing, yet it will lead to nothingness or self-destruction which is translated here as eating of dust. The fact that we all desire before we invent anything, desire becomes the key to our creativity or reproduction, which is at the same time the essence of nature or the female side; it is impeded by this curse (*"…enmity between you and the woman"*). There is going to be a total contrast between our reality and the reality that was intended. Our desire becomes our creative force, which in turn makes Adam and Eve to produce the serpent's descendants, or brood of vipers (creatures produced by man's desire).

> "To the woman he said:
> "'I will surely multiply your pain in childbearing;
> in pain you shall bring forth children.
> Your desire shall be for your husband,
> and he shall rule over you.'"

Here again the same curse resurfaces, the law of reproduction is rendered painful. The woman loses her equality with the man due to the fact that the side from which she was taken now has a greater selfish desire that will push him to no longer identify her as one body, but as two different entities. Remember that Eve was made after Adam's desire. Adam could easily recognize her as his body. With the curse, she became a separate entity. Women's equality in our society is thus to be viewed as blessing and a sign of the rising of a great nation. When man's own selfish desire overwhelms his consideration for his woman, this attitude makes him a tyrant leader in our current reality, which is a very disturbing position for him and for the whole world. Let us look at man's curse that finally concludes everything stated in previous curses.

> "To the man he said:
> 'Because you have listened to the voice of your wife
> and have eaten of the tree
> of which I commanded you.' 'You shall not eat of it,'
> cursed is the ground because of you;
> in pain you shall eat of it all the days of your life;
>
> 18 thorns and thistles it shall bring forth for you;
> and you shall eat the plants of the field.

*19 By the sweat of your face
you shall eat bread,
till you return to the ground,
for out of it you were taken;
for you are dust,
and to dust you shall return.'"*

"*Because you have listened to the voice of your wife*" is a ruling statement. Adam is being told where he went wrong. The only voice he was made to listen to was God's. The voice represents authority or supremacy. Adam listening to his wife voice was Adam regarding himself through his mirror (wife) as supreme. Remember that God viewed the act of making a woman as a permissive correctional measure to the first man's ego hiding behind his desire. It was through his wife that is nakedness was exposed but still he did not humble himself and repent. With such defiance, the Lord finally metes fair justice in condemning the man with the same curse. Man has to labor all his life to get food from the ground, and this will be his vanity till he returns to dust (death).

As a result, death became the essence of the serpent of desire with its process of twisted reality. It receives a totally different reactive stimulus from the original reality, which was the combination of breath of life and dust. The Lord God (Existence) knew that everything was part of Him and by declaring death over the human race, He meant the destruction of their original purpose and body that was made to carry out that purpose. He did not mean his existence because man's existence is eternal and part of God Himself. At death man goes back to his original state, which is dust, and his atomic configurations live on in their original state and location. This might imply "hell," the constant heat to which all matter in its unused state is subjected. It will be up to God to materially recompose them or leave them as abstract.

The remainder of the story, from verse twenty to twenty-four is more focused on the tree of Life. Before we see what this tree means, I would like to draw your attention to the fact that the Lord God (Existence) made skin garments for Adam and Eve. Even though the first man and woman had just sinned, God showed them sympathy. He still assured them of His protection against overpowering nature. But what type of skin is this? Could it be our own flesh that will imprison our soul or is it simply an animal skin? Remember that Adam had called Eve *"bone of my bones, flesh of my flesh"*; from this poetry, we affirm that the first man and woman were made of bones, flesh, blood and skin covering them. And the only option we are left with is the animal skin which might refer to atonement.

After having defined the tree of the Knowledge of Good and Evil to be the Supremacy of God; the desire in Adam and Eve, which was previously described as serpent was entrusted to act like a switch to their subordination and likeness with God by abiding to this law. The tree of Life was simply the applicability of the law. That is the reason why the whereabouts of the tree of the Knowledge of Good and Evil was not mentioned clearly to be in the middle of the Garden as was the tree of Life. It was there, but as long as Adam and Eve were still obeying God's law, the tree of the Knowledge of Good and Evil was not substantiated. Its materialization was only activated by their disobedience. The Tree of the Knowledge of Good and Evil was not itself a bad tree (Law) because the Bible implies that it played a role in the likeness with God *"Now man has become like one of us,"* and what mattered was its usage. The action of disobedience, which is itself energy, fused with another type of energy that was dormant, and stimulated it. It thus gave it an expression of deadly composition for the very nature of man, and by so disobeying, man created the devil. It has been taught in many churches around the world that God created the angel Lucifer, who fell and became Satan (the devil). However, what we have learnt from the analysis of first three chapters of the book of Genesis clearly shows us something else. Adam was the only one created as a guardian of Eden (enclosure). It is through his desire granted by God that Eve was "made". All the beasts were "formed out" of the ground. Refusing this fact is to try to shift the blame on another entity (like did Adam and Eve) rather than accepting the cunning ways of our desire.

Nowhere in the book of Genesis have we found Lucifer mentioned during the creation. However, in Ezekiel chapter 28: 1-17, a prophecy against the king of Tyre is quoted:

> "'The word of the Lord came to me: ² "Son of man, say to the ruler of Tyre, 'This is what the Sovereign Lord says:
> 'In the pride of your heart
> you say, "I am a god;
> I sit on the throne of a god
> in the heart of the seas."
> But you are a mere mortal and not a god,
> though you think you are as wise as a god.
>
> ³ Are you wiser than Daniel?
> Is no secret hidden from you?
>
> ⁴ By your wisdom and understanding
> you have gained wealth for yourself
> and amassed gold and silver
> in your treasuries.
>
> ⁵ By your great skill in trading
> you have increased your wealth,
> and because of your wealth
> your heart has grown proud.

⁶ "'Therefore this is what the Sovereign Lord says:
"'Because you think you are wise,
as wise as a god,

⁷ I am going to bring foreigners against you,
the most ruthless of nations;
they will draw their swords against your beauty and wisdom
and pierce your shining splendor.

⁸ They will bring you down to the pit,
and you will die a violent death
in the heart of the seas.

⁹ Will you then say, "I am a god,"
in the presence of those who kill you?
You will be but a mortal, not a god,
in the hands of those who slay you.

¹⁰ You will die the death of the uncircumcised
at the hands of foreigners.
I have spoken, declares the Sovereign Lord.'"

¹¹ The word of the Lord came to me: ¹² "Son of man, take up a lament concerning the king of Tyre and say to him: 'This is what the Sovereign Lord says:
"'You were the seal of perfection,
full of wisdom and perfect in beauty.

¹³ You were in Eden,
the garden of God;
every precious stone adorned you:
carnelian, chrysolite and emerald,
topaz, onyx and jasper,
lapis lazuli, turquoise and beryl.
Your settings and mountings were made of gold;
on the day you were created they were prepared.

^{14}You were anointed as a guardian cherub,
for so I ordained you.
You were on the holy mount of God;
you walked among the fiery stones.

^{15}You were blameless in your ways
from the day you were created
till wickedness was found in you.

^{16}Through your widespread trade
you were filled with violence,
and you sinned.
So I drove you in disgrace from the mount of God,
and I expelled you, guardian cherub,
from among the fiery stones.
^{17}Your heart became proud
on account of your beauty,
and you corrupted your wisdom
because of your splendor.
So I threw you to the earth;
I made a spectacle of you before kings.'"

In the above Biblical chapter though referring to the king of Tyre, we find a descriptive analysis of what exactly happened in Eden where only Adam was the guardian Cherub, and his desire to be like God was causal of his fall. Fall from where? To understand it better we will discuss it amply in the coming chapter. The serpent hiding behind the tree is simply the desire of man, His inner voice or (his ego) questioning God's declared laws (trees).

Now Adam and Eve have two large engines (the choice to make between Good and Evil) commanding the small human body. They become like God knowing Good and Evil. This was an extra essence that was not part of the original plan. They were not made to compete with their Creator, this was not their essence, and to leave them in this state was chemically and spiritually impossible. They will end up claiming to be gods but what type of gods? Surely, mortal gods as mentioned in Ezekiel 28 above.

Shrewd in His power, the Almighty decides to take them out of his original premises (the enclosure) where they had access to the switch and His protection, and He sent them off on a long journey to freedom with only their desire to rely on. The Garden's environment was no longer compatible with their essence. They lost their original purpose which was life, and they became prey to death. From that day the tree of Life was guarded by the Cherubs.

Chapter 9

Hunted by the Shadow of Desire

There is consistency in the Biblical stories about the creeping desire in man and its lethal stimulus on man's life, such as in the stories of Cain and Abel, the tower of Babel and Noah's flood etc. Man's desire did not just push him to disobey his Maker; even worse, it fostered his ego and finally made him bury His God in the very dust on which he was cursed to crawl. Man embraced the same curse to be his pinnacle to understanding the world. Preoccupied with his activities, man became an inventor, a creator of his own defined essence, which is death. He gave a form of death to everything he desired to conceive –nothing that man made last forever. By accumulating the material compositions already known to him, he then proceeded to worship himself through them. He became the god of his own creation. Most importantly, he desired to recreate man's mind and consciousness, and turn it in whichever direction he wanted and whenever he needed to do so, through conception of his own laws, and redefinition of words he personally invented and gave power to for selfish motives upon which every one of his desired actions is based: Greed, Pleasure and Honor. Man recreated himself. To him matter became primary to consciousness. He refused to recognize that consciousness is the essence of Existence. Being a materialist, man thought that a human being could reach the highest level of knowledge through his activities. He thought that there was nothing but himself and the outside world of matter. And any confrontation between him and matter will always result in two opposite forces which are the destruction of the old and the birth of the new. It is the coward who fails to stick to the fight or who cannot start one, and then creates "God" as an excuse, he thinks. The idea of God was always linked to man's vulnerability in the face of natural phenomena. Disasters were causative to the idea of a supreme being whenever man could not shield himself from them. It is a materialistic individual who relies on man's reason and inquires about their roots through cross examination of causes and effects. Once he has analyzed the situations and summarized what he has seen and foresees in the future, then he can use the experiences accumulated to make sure that every situation is under control. However, this has never been the case. Man does not master any situation though visibly some seem to. Why?

The answer is that by transgressing the divine law, a great impairment in the natural balance occurred that could be linked to man's activities. Prior to his transgression, man was in charge of all living things. He then could communicate with water, mountains, animals, fish, trees, all things. Some of you may wonder does a mountain or water speak? No, they do not speak with words, but they were made in such a way to react to our will and everything that reacts to our will is conscious and thus can communicate with us. Otherwise we would not be able to hit a nail with a hammer. Alternatively, if you are a Christian you probably know that Jesus spoke to the storm and it obeyed him. Due to Adam's sin, nature now obeys and listens to God only. It no longer communicates with us humans. In electronics there is such a term for communication with the different programmable components on the printed circuit board (PCB). Man's single action was capable of navigating perfectly through the web of the laws of nature without disturbing its harmonious balance. There were no accidents or inaccuracies in the movement of masses until man sinned.

To understand the magnitude of the instability caused by this sin let me take you through the hurricane's embryo and the wisdom in it. According to Kerry Emanuel, Professor of Atmospheric Science working at the Massachusetts Institute of Technology, speaking during an interview on earth, atmospheric and planetary sciences on the British Broadcasting Cooperation; he mentioned that most hurricanes in the Atlantic begin in very small atmospheric disturbances in a jet stream that flows from East to West over sub-Saharan Africa. These disturbances are called an easterly wave and can be caused by anything. It can be a little girl who simply found herself playing in the sand, and triggered a small dust devil that perturbs the atmosphere downstream. The easterly waves create a system of turbulent edges that go on to develop into a cluster of thunder storms that travel West across the African continent to encounter the warm tropical waters of the Atlantic. These thunder storms appear to become better organized and begin to rotate around each other until the rotation rate increases and the storm becomes more vigorous. The wind continues to increase and finally the storm rapidly gathers strength and develops into a hurricane that feeds itself from the warm moist air coming from the Atlantic. The heat starts coming out of the ocean, and the hurricane heat engine converts that heat energy that comes from the ocean into mechanical energy of the wind to give the storm full strength. When the wind reaches seventy to eighty miles per hour, the storm develops an eye surrounded by an eye wall which is caused by the intensity of the heat of the water and the strength of the wind and suddenly damage is done on the land. Now you can understand how a small amount of dust caused by anything as the stamping feet of a little child can travel four thousand miles across the Atlantic and cause catastrophe on the U.S. coastland. Amazing is it not it? But this is how a single action of a human being can travel through the web of natural laws and cause an avalanche of damages that will affect the world continuously and transform it from day to day until its total destruction.

Chapter 10

Our Actions Versus Our Desire and Their Reality Implications

The word action is one of the most vaguely defined words in the history of humankind because it embodies accountability and judgment. So there is a reason why everyone needed to arrive at their own meaning of what one must do to appear right or wrong. But in some of the common definitions, action is defined as doing something. In Latin action means also legal proceeding (*lis*) or battle (*pugna*).

The allegorical meaning of the word "action" is the expressed shifting of energy. As you may not know, our universe is an open system that continuously interacts with its environment. Thus said, its interactions can take the forms of energy such as information or materials and transfer them into and out of the system. Energy itself is defined as the ability to do work. Man has described different forms of energy, such as: radiation, biomass energy, black energy that pushes galaxies apart, and others. But you may never have heard about the behavioral energy that is expressed more through our characters. Like any form of energy, our behavioral energy is transferred through our motivation, which is the activation of goal oriented behavior. Our motivation can be intrinsic or extrinsic depending upon whether our desire for change comes from within us or from external forces.

Remember that having said that we are man-made man, this means that we perform most actions not because we desire them from within ourselves, but because there are external forces that compel us to action in order to satisfy other people's desires. We can apply our conscience correctly whenever we are moved to do something by asking ourselves: why are we doing this? This question itself will have a tremendous impact on our action and accountability. The Latin expression: *"actus me invito factus non est meus actus."* which means, *"the act done by me against my will is not my act,"* conveys a powerful message with respect to the categorization of actions, understanding of the motif, and accountability. The action does not make the person guilty unless the mind is guilty *"actus non facit reum nisi mens sit rea."* There is a huge responsibility on our mind and its conscience screen to use their given capability to detect the motivations of our actions, whether intrinsic or extrinsic. Most motivations take shape through a process called attention, interest, desire, action (AIDA). I invite you to keep in mind the cunning way that the serpent of desire duped Eve in the Garden of Eden as we develop the AIDA system, which is well known by economists. Note that "AIDIA," which is the advanced form of AIDA used in philosophy, will be clearly explained in chapter thirteen with respect to "success versus our reality."

Internal or external forms of energy rouse our "attention" through our five senses, and once one or some of these senses are tuned, they perceive the energy as sensory energy. The mind, with its conscious filter that plays the role of a combination transducer, picks up this sensory energy and translates it into feelings or emotional energy; we then become "interested" in what our senses are tuned to and relate to them. A combination transducer is a device acting as a sensor that combines two functions: it detects and creates action. For example, a typical ultrasonic transducer switches back and forth many times a second between acting as an actuator to produce ultrasonic waves, and acting as a sensor to detect ultrasonic waves.

Most of the time, instead of conveying the emotional energy back to the combination transducer that is made up of mind and conscience in order to match the energy with the laws of nature to produce wisdom, instead emotional energy, in form feelings, acts immediately. Due to its urgency intensified by our desire over the mind, the emotional energy bridges itself with the sensory organs and transforms its energy into "unscreened" mechanical or moving energy: action. As noticed in the above description, the mind and its conscience screen (combination transducer) are excluded in their second role of processing the action or are underestimated by our desire (Devil). When this occurs our actions become intentional and devoid of judgments. We can have an intentional action devoid of good judgments but we cannot have a good judgment devoid of intention. People act intentionally to satisfy their cravings, by the time they act conscientiously it becomes for a common good.

Most of our actions are framed as thoughts and it is only when these thoughts are complete and ready to be executed that their purposes start, and the latter last for perpetuity being transformed from one form of energy to another, even after we have long passed. Once an action is hatched, it discharges a permanent energy that navigates in and out of our universe, and may be converted into anything if met with a unique stimulus that complements it at its appropriate reactive temperature, time, speed and location. I know that this is the truth by experiences and by analyzing the parable of the sower in Matthew 13:3-9.

> *"Then he told them many things in parables, saying: "A farmer went out to sow his seed. 4 As he was scattering the seed, some fell along the path, and the birds came and ate it up. 5 Some fell on rocky places, where it did not have much soil. It sprang up quickly, because the soil was shallow. 6 But when the sun came up, the plants were scorched, and they withered because they had no root. 7 Other seed fell among thorns, which grew up and choked the plants. 8 Still other seed fell on good soil, where it produced a crop—a hundred, sixty or thirty times what was sown. 9 He who has ears, let him hear."*

The fate of the seed was much more determined by the sower's way of scattering it, where he was positioned, the type of ground and soil the seed fell on, the speed and the overall temperature. Our actions are seeds and every time we do something, the results are determined much more by who we are first, our location, and the forces around us.

Due to the constant transformation of behavioral energy, our reality becomes incomprehensible and uncertain; we are unable to predict the future with accuracy. Even if we act morally, we are uncertain what trajectory our discharged energy (actions) will take, what will further stimulate it, and what its next essence will be: Ecclesiastes 6:12: *"For who knows what is good for a person in life, during the few and meaningless days they pass through like a shadow? Who can tell them what will happen under the sun after they are gone?"*

Ecclesiastes 8:14: *"There is something else meaningless that occurs on earth: the righteous who get what the wicked deserve, and the wicked who get what the righteous deserve. This too, I say, is meaningless."*

Today's world, its people and their behavioral energy, which in this case can be called cultures and customs, are all products of previous intrinsic or extrinsic motivations of people who lived before us. Their actions or behavioral energy went through several transformations to act as catalysts to what we are today. To have a good Biblical look at this I would like to refer again to the Eden story.

At the time God forbade Adam and Eve to eat from the tree of the Knowledge of Good and Evil, which we found to be a usurpation of His supremacy, He knew that it was a form of energy that was to be avoided if they guided themselves according to the law. The energy was a good energy and was constant. Their disobedience transformed the constant energy into another form which was not there but was a possibility through disobedience. Let us say that one will remain one if nothing is added to or subtracted from it. As long as this law is preserved, one will always be one. But when the law is violated other numbers less or more than one will appear that were not observable but would exist if the law was violated. Throughout the curse of desire (serpent) God refers to the enmity between the woman's descendants and those of the serpent. Full understanding of this curse lies in the fact that the sons of man (Eve's descendants) will use their "desire" to create some of the actions (descendants of the serpent)—their motives do not matter—that are themselves forms of energy. These energies will travel through our universe that has laws acting as combination transducers that have themselves a bi-dimensional function of detecting motives and recreating actions. Natural laws (The combination transducers), the universe's mind or central system, detect the trajectory of our actions and their motives and transform them into physical processes. These physical processes or phenomena will not always be pleasant; this is expressed by the words: *"he shall bruise your head, and you shall bruise his heel."* I know that most Christians talk about to this portion of the Bible to be referring to Jesus Christ. I definitely agree with that because of the fact that He epitomized this verse through His mastery in overcoming human's desire; I will develop this subject in detail in upcoming pages as we reveal the truth about Jesus Christ.

Research in neuroscience has shown that our thoughts are biochemical and electrical. They are real matter, and our mind consists photons of light held within an electromagnetic field.

We are electromagnetic beings as seen previously who emits and receive forms of energy whenever we interact with other people. These forms of energy vibrate in a certain way in the universe according to their chemical composition, time and space. Once these impulses are decoded by natural laws (combination transducers), these laws react immediately with other existing forms of energy. These reactions or actions can be anything from temperature changes, volcanos, movement of masses, or a dog fight, to the creation of forms of energy called angels and demons. Probably by now you are shaking your head in disagreement, but I invite you to consider the following, as we decipher the Bible wisdom piece by piece: In Genesis chapter 1: 1-2 it is written:

> *"In the beginning, God created the heavens and the earth. 2 The earth was without form and void, and darkness was over the face of the deep. And the Spirit of God was hovering over the face of the waters"*

These two verses reveal to us that some energy forms existed prior to the creation of the heavens and earth. They were not created; they were part of God but not equal to him.

The first form of energy is the Spirit, the second was air implied by the verb hovering, and waters were the third. You may wonder why air and waters? The answer lies in the combination of the first verse and verses six to nine when God decided to create an expanse in the midst of the waters to separate waters from waters. One was named heaven and the other earth (the dry land and seas). Air and Water were the infinite matter that was part of God and from which other forms of matter were or are still derived. The air was right above the waters or enveloped them. When the waters were separated the air remained and from the waters that were above plus air, heaven was made and everything else in it, including our galaxies of stars originated from the same combination of waters above plus air. From the waters that were under the heavens plus air, man, beasts, plants, fish, and all living things were made. That is the reason why you find four elements in all matter: air, water, fire or light, and earth. The substantiation of forms of light such as the sun, the moon and the stars was made to regulate time and seasons in order to help man calculate his days. Prior to them, light and darkness in more infinite forms existed and were part of Existence.

As we have already seen, God, who is Existence, has His essence in His consciousness, which is the perfect balance that controls the universe and its laws, and is cognizant of all essences including its own and that of all matter and uses it to satisfy His will and His unfathomable needs. This Spirit was the primary and only constant energy that was conscious of itself and of its other energy forms. When God decided to share a part of Himself with the first man by making him conscious, it was the most divine act of a loving God, which was accompanied by the blessing of reproduction. Man was given the privilege to tap into the same constant energy to reproduce other forms of energy according to well-defined terms and conditions, not by his own will. However, after eating the forbidden fruit, the results of which were known by God, who had put laws in place as preventive measures that give our worship expression, man produced a form of energy that was not there but existed because its configurations were not yet combined to cause it to function. It is there in Eden that an opposing form of energy to man's essence was born: Satan (the adversary) or the devil (the slanderer), attribute of desire.

When man sinned, the formula to reverse the process (return to the tree of Life) was guarded from him; hence his conscious ability became limited, evolving around his desire. By applying a well-intentioned desire, man was capable of reproducing righteous forms of energy; but, by using his selfish energy, ego or evil desire, other forces were created (evil). Ever since, this duality (Good and Evil) will forever haunt man's nature.

Each of Adam's descendants who acted according to a well-intentioned desire was accepted by God to be His son or a form of His energy; the first of these was Abel. The ill-intentioned, like Cain, emanated from man's ego and was called "son or daughter" of man as based on man's gender.

The fact that both of these forms of energy were reflected by Adam's first descendants, the well-intentioned desire, no matter how long it lasted, always ended by being coupled with man's ego. That is why the observation is made in Genesis 6: 1-3 "... *My spirit shall not abide in man forever for his flesh...*" Man cannot remain good forever, he always succumbs at last.

From that day of Noah, man's years were shortened; there was no need to lengthen a good man's years only to discover that he at last succumbs to sin. If you have good discernment, you will see that the statement that the spirit shall not abide in man simply means the spirit of God cannot remain stable or reside in man forever. This implies that even a righteous man, if given enough time in this world of sin, will end up offending God's spirit. The Lord God who possesses all energies and knows their essences and communicates with them, and who knows and understands the stimuli that can create and destroy them, had put in place a process at the beginning of time that is reversibly restoring His oneness with man. This restoration was embedded in the consciousness of mankind's mind in connection with his thoughts and the way he acts on them. His thoughts toward his activities were forms of energy emission that were transformed into other forms that substantiated man's approaches to particular conceptions that are also series of forms of energy. Some viewed natural occurrences as challenges that man should strive to solve. Others conceived them as gods and for some these were signs of only one God. These concepts, being also forms of energy, continue to play a role in the restoration of God's oneness with man.

Chapter 11

The Begining of Restoration at Babel

Genesis 11: 1-9

"1 Now the whole earth had one language and the same words. 2 And as people migrated from the east, they found a plain in the land of Shinar and settled there. 3 And they said to one another, 'Come, let us make bricks, and burn them thoroughly.' And they had brick for stone, and bitumen for mortar. 4 Then they said, 'Come, let us build ourselves a city and a tower with its top in the heavens, and let us make a name for ourselves, lest we be dispersed over the face of the whole earth.' 5 And the Lord came down to see the city and the tower, which the children of man had built. 6 And the Lord said, 'Behold, they are one people, and they have all one language, and this is only the beginning of what they will do. And nothing that they propose to do will now be impossible for them. 7 Come, let us go down and there confuse their language, so that they may not understand one another's speech.' 8 So the Lord dispersed them from there over the face of all the earth and they left off building the city. 9 Therefore its name was called Babel, because there the Lord confused the language of all the earth. And from there the Lord dispersed them over the face of all the earth."

The Reality Of Our Chemical Composition and Our Spirituality

Many believe that God confused people's language at Babel so that we have thousands of them today. But looking closely at this story we find a labyrinth of a much greater divine wisdom. Before we plunge into the story, I would like you to know that our mind's thoughts, being complete actions in their primitive stage, thus too being energy forms, use our senses as the conduit to align themselves with the outside world's energy forms. After processing these sensory forms of energy in the consciousness and mind, the latter reuse these same senses to redistribute the transformed energy of the mind back into the world. The main source of these energies arises during our friction with nature through our activities. The best distributor of this transformed energy is language in all its forms: spoken words, visual gestures and writings, touch, even smell which is called scent communication, which can move us emotionally and create desire without a single word being spoken.

In Genesis 9, God's covenant with Noah is detailed as follows:

> *"[1] Then God blessed Noah and his sons, saying to them, 'Be fruitful and increase in number and fill the earth. [2] The fear and dread of you will fall on all the beasts of the earth, and on all the birds in the sky, on every creature that moves along the ground, and on all the fish in the sea; they are given into your hands. [3] Everything that lives and moves about will be food for you. Just as I gave you the green plants, I now give you everything.'*
>
> *[4] 'But you must not eat meat that has its lifeblood still in it. [5] And for your lifeblood I will surely demand an accounting. I will demand an accounting from every animal. And from each human being, too, I will demand an accounting for the life of another human being.'*

⁶ 'Whoever sheds human blood,
by humans shall their blood be shed;
for in the image of God
has God made mankind.

⁷ As for you, be fruitful and increase in number; multiply on the earth and increase upon it.'

⁸ Then God said to Noah and to his sons with him: ⁹ 'I now establish my covenant with you and with your descendants after you ¹⁰ and with every living creature that was with you the birds, the livestock and all the wild animals, all those that came out of the ark with you every living creature on earth. ¹¹ I establish my covenant with you: Never again will all life be destroyed by the waters of a flood; never again will there be a flood to destroy the earth.'

¹² And God said, 'this is the sign of the covenant I am making between me and you and every living creature with you, a covenant for all generations to come: ¹³ I have set my rainbow in the clouds, and it will be the sign of the covenant between me and the earth. ¹⁴ Whenever I bring clouds over the earth and the rainbow appears in the clouds, ¹⁵ I will remember my covenant between me and you and all living creatures of every kind. Never again will the waters become a flood to destroy all life. ¹⁶ Whenever the rainbow appears in the clouds, I will see it and remember the everlasting covenant between God and all living creatures of every kind on the earth.'

¹⁷ So God said to Noah, 'This is the sign of the covenant I have established between me and all life on the earth.'

The Sons of Noah

¹⁸ The sons of Noah who came out of the ark were Shem, Ham and Japheth. (Ham was the father of Canaan.) ¹⁹ These were

the three sons of Noah, and from them came the people who were scattered over the whole earth.

[20] Noah, a man of the soil, proceeded to plant a vineyard. [21] When he drank some of its wine, he became drunk and lay uncovered inside his tent. [22] Ham, the father of Canaan, saw his father naked and told his two brothers outside. [23] But Shem and Japheth took a garment and laid it across their shoulders; then they walked in backward and covered their father's naked body. Their faces were turned the other way so that they would not see their father naked.

[24] When Noah awoke from his wine and found out what his youngest son had done to him, [25] he said,

'Cursed be Canaan!
The lowest of slaves
will he be to his brothers.'

[26] He also said,
'Praise be to the Lord, the God of Shem!
May Canaan be the slave of Shem.

[27] May God extend Japheth's territory;
may Japheth live in the tents of Shem,
and may Canaan be the slave of Japheth.'

[28] After the flood Noah lived 350 years. [29] Noah lived a total of 950 years, and then he died."

Prior to building the tower of Babel, the Bible speaks of a world after the flood where Noah and his family were the sole survivors. The Lord God blessed Noah to be fruitful and He reconfirmed man's dominion over nature, but with one rule: "not to eat flesh with its life, meaning 'Blood.'" This was a second earthly covenant after that with Adam's. Though this covenant was sustained by the "law of blood restriction," Noah was still naked before God as was Adam. He was exposed and vulnerable but protected by God. However, Noah's desire for wine paved the way for Ham to uncover his father's vulnerability. There was an intention to breach the covenant, but this time it was not willful on Noah's part. It was *"actus non facit reum nisi mens sit rea."* *"The act done by me against my will is not my act."* An action does not make the person guilty unless the mind is. Ham wanted to push Noah to break the law and went as Eve did to Adam to tell his brothers to partake in the sin; but his brothers Shem and Japheth, however, refused. Instead they took a position (a garment) to offer human's protection and protected their father and themselves. The fact that they were walking backward while offering protection was the ultimate way to avoid eye contact, which can be so appealing to surrender to Ham's temptation. This is something that Eve did not do when tempted by Satan: "And when the woman *saw* that the tree was good for food, and that it was a *delight to the eyes...*" When Noah awoke from his wine, he was told of his son's intention and, knowing that intentions are complete actions, he was moved to curse his son's descendants, the Canaanites, while the other two brothers were blessed. This notion that intentions equal actions was well known by Jesus Christ when talking to the Pharisees in Matthew 5: 28: *"but I tell you that anyone who looks at a woman lustfully has already committed adultery with her in his heart."*

It was only after this event that the Bible describes nations descended from Noah. Looking closely at Genesis 10: 5 when the sons of Japheth are described, we see that *"from these the coastland peoples spread in their lands, each with his own language, by their clans, in their nations."* We can conclude that people started to speak different languages prior to the tower of Babel. Then why does the Bible choose chapter 11 to tell the event of the tower? Does chapter 11 contradict chapter 10? No, the Bible is far from contradicting itself; instead it reveals once more, allegorically, a divine intervention that has knitted every fiber of our life's activities since.

Because language is the expression of thoughts, then it is also the essence of every action or thought. Thus, "people who speak the same language" means those who act the same because they share the same ideology. An ideology is defined to be a set of ideas that defines one's goals, expectations, and actions. It can be a vision of a nation or a way of looking at things. *"The whole earth had one language and the same words"* simply means that the whole earth had the same ideology, way of perceiving things, the same applicability of their thoughts and the targeted end. What was their ideology? Verse 4 explains: Then they said: *"Come, let us build ourselves a city and a tower with its top in the heavens, and let us make a name for ourselves, lest we be dispersed over the face of the whole earth."* The whole goal was egocentric. The people wanted to make a name for themselves; they desired honor and veneration. This was the language or thought of all the earth's people. They were scared that a time would come when they would be dispersed but it would mean nothing if they were united in their actions. This honor and oneness of thoughts was supposed to be achieved through their activities, at which they persevered day and night. God was no longer in the picture. The concept of a Creator was forgotten, his sovereignty was threatened; it was only the honor of man through his activities, which are described as building a city with the tower, which is represented here as an authority or governance over the city that prevailed then. Contrary to some opinions that suggest that ancient people wanted to build a tower that was supposed to reach the heaven to worship the sun and the moon, we can reasonably now prove that this was not the case.

The whole world was atheist; people trusted themselves and their work. When God saw their actions and intentions, He realized that His sovereignty was at stake, and the whole human race was moving towards extinction because of its sin. This was not God's intention when he made His covenant with Noah. Being Love, He had to intervene to rescue man from self-destruction. To accomplish that, He confused their language, implying their common understanding of their atheist ideology. Unable to understand each other in their efforts to build an atheist society, some gave up and set out for a new place till they were dispersed over the face of all the earth. When this misunderstanding occurred, it did not mean that some people simply turned to monotheism and became comfortable with it or with one another. Instead, their theism was filled with different ideologies, where anything or anyone could be called god. This type of theism paved the way for the atheist's plan of action to better control man using his fear of a Creator. That is why, philosophically, the concept of God's existence is believed to have emanated from man's imagination when confronted with misfortunes in the discovery of the universe through his activities. With time this idea evolved; the shrewd egocentric man hijacked the concept that was already a reflection of man's weakness to formulate theories that would misuse man's apprehension for the benefits of his selfish desire. These theories were nothing other than human disciplines or science. It is through these theories that man redefined many of his thoughts and words to conquer other humans. In transparent philosophical principles science is viewed as a set of skills used by people to produce solutions to problems in order to advance themselves politically and socially while hiding behind the erected walls of religion. One might say that scientists do not hide behind religion, but remember that a religion involves devotional observances, and often containing moral rules that govern the conduct of human's affairs. At the tower of Babel, humans were devotional to knowing their activities (sciences). Working for the honor of man and him alone is considered to be a sacred thing in our modern sciences, thus, making our generation the most idolatrous in the history of mankind. It is not all scientists who work to honor themselves. There are those who have dedicated their entire hard work and discoveries to honor their Creator.

In the time of the tower of Babel, those who held to their original plan to stay together while focusing solely on their human activities to better themselves as super humans while denying God evolved into those we would today refer to as "communists." However, those who used religion and man's fear of God as their shield in order to advance their political agenda, while still focusing on selfish activities, became known as "capitalists."

These first two branches of the Babel inhabitants that survived in different types of governments (ideologies) throughout the course of history had an even more hidden agenda. They hoped to revive their ancient plan of superseding God so that by exposing each other's agendas through clashes, they would make common people who are already in weak position turn their backs on God and refute the idea of His involvement in human affairs. The friction between the two factions would cause such a bitter and twisted view of life in order to prompt the conscious man to question the authenticity of a God who is Love amid life's cataclysms. Today's scientific knowledge is based totally on man's efforts to understand the world and uplift his ego rather than to give glory to the Originator of all existence. This truly was the language or the thoughts at the time of the tower of Babel. Modern philosophical thought that is inclusive of ancient philosophy is identical in that both deny or distort the concept of God (Existence). Everything ever invented through science has been a defensive reaction rather than an offensive action towards the needs that nature imposes on us. This means that man has never invented an object that operates outside the context of the universe. This attempt would be impossible. In order that man would fully understand his place in the universe, God had to restore man' oneness with Him, and for that He called upon Abraham, whose name was then Abram, a name that was changed when God changed Abram's life (essence).

Chapter 12

Abraham's Essence

Later in life, Abraham left his country Ur on a divine mission of restoration between God and man. He accepted the responsibility that comes with accountability, and based on his attitude God promised to make Abraham a great nation, and said that through him, all the earth would be blessed. Abraham's total separation: from his country, his brothers, and from his father's house, was symbolic of something unique that had nothing to do with his family bloodline, but that would be the hallmark of everything that Abraham would become. It was supposed to be a very emotional separation, but he was prepared to face his feelings with reason. But where was he supposed to go? The Lord God ("Existence") had told him of a promised land where he would dwell. Being a blessing to all the earth entailed that everything he thought or acted upon would be blessed. All his needs would be met.

Genesis 12:2-3 says *"I will bless those who bless you and him who dishonors you I will curse..."*

This simple and clear sentence reveals the quickest way to anyone's prosperity or failure: genuinely bless Abraham and you will be blessed;

curse him and you will be cursed. I know you are probably wondering how you can bless someone who died thousands of years ago. Does it not sound like my aunty telling me to venerate my dead ancestors instead of crucified Jesus? Your question will be answered as we develop Abraham's essence.

Abraham had a divine character of gratitude that made him God's ideal choice for His mission. The Lord God showed Abraham Canaan and promised to give him and his descendants the land. Remember, Canaanites were the descendants of Ham who uncovered his father Noah's nudity and was cursed. So Abraham's presence there might alter the situation.

As Abraham arrived in Canaan, he was faced with a special problem; his wife Sarai (whom God renamed Sarah), who was barren, wanted him to have an heir. Barrenness is a condition, as detailed in my childhood's story in Africa, considered a curse from the gods rather than a biological state. A barren woman cannot yield anything of value and for that she is not allowed to work in the field. In Roman mythology *"Lua"* was the goddess of barrenness to whom all spoils of wars were ritually burnt as sacrifices to her. This implies that a barren woman was looked upon as spoil devoid of beauty and value. How could it be possible for a couple chosen by God to form a great nation to have no offspring? The only alternative his legal wife Sarah had was to suggest that Abraham take her maidservant, Hagar, who joined them when they passed through Egypt. Hagar was from pharaoh's house and was given to Sarah. Abraham took Hagar as his second wife and from that union he produced Ishmael at the age of eighty-six. Ishmael is a combination of two words: "Listen" and "Elohim" ("God" in Hebrew) —"God listens." This name is going to be the essence that supports the child's life.

However, because Sarah did not listen to God's promise that she would have a child; a message that was embedded in God's promise to make Abraham into a great nation, Ishmael was issued from "Sarah's desire" to please her husband Abraham. Though God listened to her, the behavior (serpent of desire) turned back to bite her. She was looked on with contempt by Hagar, her own servant. It was not God's desire but Sarah's that the Lord allowed to be fulfilled. Realizing her mistake, she turned back to Abraham for comfort, but the latter's response is tinted with a tone of accountability: *"Behold your servant is in your power; do to her as you please."* From that response, Sarah dealt harshly with her then-pregnant maidservant, who decided to flee before Ishmael's birth. As she left, the Lord's angel (energy given essence) appeared and described to her the purpose behind the life of the child to whom she's going to give birth:

> *"A wild donkey of a man, His hand against everyone and everyone's hand against him and he shall dwell over against all his kinsmen."*

Why this description of someone's essence? The key word that we all should look at is "wild." Decoding this word will greatly enlighten us to the character of a nation that people so long misunderstood.

The word wild is known to be the antonym of domesticated or tamed. Its other meanings can be "that which does not take the intended course," "erratic," and "uncontrolled" and this is how we stereotype it in relation to man' intentions. But let us look at another word associated with "wild": "Wilderness," which should not be confused with wildness that comes from wilderness. Wilderness is an environment on earth untouched yet by human activities. It can also be described as the most intact, undisturbed place, one that humans can never control. So Ishmael, being a wild donkey, whose hand is against everyone, means no man will be able to understand him, his ideologies (thoughts) or energy. He will stay original and untamed by man's influences when it comes to his nature; not even his relatives will understand him. He will be isolated too; he will not mingle with others because the latter will have difficulty understanding him. Only the Lord God knows why He put Ishmael in that position. However, history informs us that through Ishmael another monotheistic faith was born (Islam) among Arabs who are recorded to be Ishmael's descendants.

Thus, it appears that even though Ishmael would not be understood he would be the progenitor of a great nation because the Lord God blessed him.

> "...I will surely multiply your offspring...You shall call his name Ishmael... And he will be a wild man; his hand will be against every man and every man's hand against him..."
> (Genesis 16:10 -12)

Chapter 13

The Impossible Made Possible

Thirteen years after the birth of Ishmael, God tells Abraham, who is then ninety-nine years old, that Sarah, his ninety years old wife is going to become pregnant. By *"Lex Naturalis"* the law of nature, this is not possible; Sarah cannot conceive at that age. But obviously this is for normal humans; God's laws are not natural to God, they are Him though not equal to Him and they will execute that from which they are consciously made:

> *"Your wife Sarah will bear you a son, and you will name him Isaac. I will establish my covenant with him as an eternal covenant to his descendants after him. And as for Ishmael... I have bless him and I will make him fruitful and will increase him exceedingly. He will become the father of twelve princes and I will make him into a great nation. But I will establish my covenant with Isaac who Sarah will bear to you at this time next year."* (Genesis 17:19-21).

With Isaac's birth Abraham's mission was secured because when Isaac was forty and his father one hundred and forty years old, Isaac married Rebecca, who finally became pregnant with twins twenty years later.

The twins were fighting even in the womb – it is a complicated pregnancy. When Esau and Jacob were born there was contention between them.

Although they were twins, Jacob and Esau had totally different behavioral energies and were also physically different. The Bible describes Esau to be a skillful hunter, a man of action who had hairy skin, while his brother Jacob was smooth-skinned and liked farming. These two characters are complete opposites. To be a man of action can be dangerous because most of our actions derive from feelings or emotions (desire) that blur the reason that contains our conscience, the filter through which feelings should be channeled and scrutinized before action. Finally, the time arrived when Isaac was old and blind, and he decided to give each of his sons a blessing. He wanted to give a much greater blessing to Esau, his first-born, who possessed the energy that he inherited from his father Abraham to carry out God's mission.

There was a problem, however, something was done in the past that the mother was aware of, and it helped her decide which of her children's personalities was most appealing. Esau did not value his birthright, to the point that he sold it to Jacob for a lentil stew. This was a sign of a severe weakness that would compromise God's mission, a mission much greater than a simple human craving over something (desire).

It was clear that Esau did not really want the position of the first-born, with its obligation to carry on his father's mission. However, he wanted the blessing of wealth and power that comes with it. When Rebecca realized that the blessing had to go to Jacob, her favorite and the one who consented to handle his father's mission, she covered

Jacob's arms with a goat skin so they would feel hairy like Esau's. Isaac, being blind, was fooled into blessing Jacob while Esau was out hunting to catch something for his father's favorite dinner. Isaac finally realized that Jacob was representing himself as Esau; he sensed through Jacob's voice that he had been tricked:

> "The voice is Jacob's voice, but the hands are the hands of Esau." (Genesis 27:22).

There are people who feel that Jacob cheated by repeatedly lying to Isaac when he wanted to find out if he was truly Esau. On a spiritual level, when you sell your birthright, you sell also your essence, which is the whole of your being. You, your name and the whole energy in you, makes up what you are (your usefulness or purpose in life), and selling your usefulness to someone is to sell your whole identity. During an awareness campaign about female sex slaves and victims of human trafficking in South Africa, there was a point that I raised to explain the difference in severity between selling oneself as a human commodity and being sold as one. By selling yourself there is a deliberate action of disposing of what you are made for; it is giving away your entire essence into the hands of someone else who then has complete power over you. He can even go so far as to alter your essence completely by taking your life which you sold to him. But if you are taken *forcefully* or lured into slavery, you have not yet lost your essence and no matter what and how long it takes you, as long as you are alive, you can still regain your identity. This is the blueprint of every individual who was or still is coerced into any kind of slavery.

Jacob's claim to Esau's birthright was spiritually true and legitimate, not a lie.

Esau, who embodies the behavioral energy of desire, realized that he had just been cheated by his brother, who by his reason knew the value of what Esau despised, and Esau decided to kill Jacob. Rebecca saw his intentions and advised Jacob to flee.

You will realize that the blessing bestowed upon Jacob included riches and authority over all nations, but was bound with a rule of not marrying a Canaanite woman. This act was the only stimulus that could irreversibly alter the composition of Jacob's blessing that was his new essence given by his parents. On the other hand, Esau, who was already interested in a Canaanite woman, thought that taking a Canaanite woman for his wife might have contributed to him not being fit for his father's blessing. Because of that he goes on to take the wife of his uncle Ishmael, and through his descendants with this woman, he gives rise to "Edomites" or "nation of Edom" as the Bible calls it. To understand today who these people are, let us turn to Genesis again.

In Genesis 27:39-40 we found the words of Isaac when he was pushed incessantly by his son Esau to bless him also:

> *"Behold [away from] the fatness of the earth shall your dwelling be, and [away from] the dew of heaven on high. 40 By your sword you shall live and you shall serve your brother; but when you grow restless you shall break his yoke from your neck."*

Some translations do not interpret correctly the Hebrew preposition "of" which means *"here from"* or *"away from."* The other thing we know is that in verse 37 of the same chapter Isaac made it clear to Esau that he could not give him what was already given to Jacob. So Esau received the opposite of Jacob's blessing: a "curse" and this explains why the words are the same but contrasted by the preposition "away from" that means at a distance, not close to. However, this curse was revelatory of what Esau and his descendants are today.

Looking into the story we see that Esau is not given the fatness of the earth and that he will be kept away from the dew of heaven.

These two words are complementary to each other in that Esau was denied the produce of the earth and the dew that makes its growth possible. As dew is beneficial to summer crops, so is true knowledge and wisdom to man's activities. But the question is how he is going to survive without the fatness of the earth and dew. The Bible is clear: *"By your sword you shall live and serve your brother."*

In this particular sentence the scriptures tell us that Esau will be waging war to provide for himself while also serving or working for Jacob. But the time will come when he will become restless; and the weight of Jacob's authority will weigh too heavily on him and he will decide to break free. Who are Esau's people today? Before we find out let us see what became of Jacob.

Jacob did what his parents advised him to do, and married two of Laban's daughters. Lea, the first wife, gave him ten offspring, while Rachel gave birth to two children called Joseph and Benjamin who were the most valued children among the twelve. When Jacob decided to leave his father-in-law's house due to some problems he encountered while working for him, the angel of the Lord told him to go back to his father's house, but he was afraid of Esau who might be lingering in the desert with mighty people to kill him as he had promised years before. However, before he thought of a plan to avoid meeting Esau, someone important met him. After wrestling all night with an unknown person for the sake of being blessed, Jacob's hip was dislocated. Admiring his determination, the unknown person blessed Jacob by giving him the new name of *"Israel,"* which became his new Essence. Jacob had to prove his willpower to achieve something of value through a painful struggle with the unknown person that the Bible describes as "God" in Genesis Chapter 35:10; thereafter, Jacob deserved his privileges.

The meaning of the new name was bellicose: *"...for you have striven with God and with men and have prevailed."* When looking closely at the allegorical meaning of Jacob's new essence, it exposes not just how Israel will struggle to carry out God' mission, but also the power of repentance on Israel's side and forgiveness on God's side, which will always be available for Israel till he wins the battle. Israel's struggle with men will occur every time he is executing God's mission of restoration, and his struggle with God will occur when he violates his mission to indulge himself in activities that glorify him and not God.

Thus, we see it is a one-front war in the sense that it will all depend on his behavioral energy toward man's activities as God uses him in restoring His covenant with men. This essence has tinted the life of the Israelites throughout history in every country in which they have sojourned.

The Israelis' reality has been the most amazing and transcendental reality that goes beyond description, but lies within the boundaries of God's provisional action. We are all witnessing the rise of a little nation that has surmounted the waves of assimilation as it still stands perceptibly frail between God and men.

Contrary to Jacob, who became Israel, Esau's essence stayed the same and he was already married to a Canaan woman, though he later decided to take his uncle Ishmael's wife. He lost his father's pure blood lineage. There was assimilation in his life that affected his essence.

As I was writing this book, I had a chance to speak to some Jewish and Christian friends who referred to the descendants of Esau as residing in Bozrah. Most of them said they were the Romans, Germans, and finally the western power. But we have said that there is nothing of a pure bloodline of Esau left due to his assimilation with other nations.

So where can they be and how can they be identified? The Bible did give us a clue: *"You will serve your brother and by the sword you shall live."* Someone who is serving his brother should be near him and associated with him. The served and the servant should live under the same roof, or institutions and laws should be put in place so that these norms prevail and distance does not prevent the served from being served and the servant from serving. Today we know that just a small number of Jews have made it to Israel while many remain in their diaspora, which entails that both in Israel and throughout the world in the diaspora, many Esau's descendants may be found. Their identification can only be achieved through a close analysis of actions that are the products of their desire. Remember a desire plays the role of a talking serpent hiding behind a tree (God's law), and it uses the AIDA concept (attention, interest, desire and action) to attract its prey.

"By your sword you shall live." The word "sword" brings to mind a bladed weapon used predominantly for cutting or thrusting during wars. Currently these edged weapons are not often used because they have been replaced by much more sophisticated guns. But there is a relation that should be anticipated between the "sword" and "money" here.

In the Gospel of Luke, chapter 22:36, Jesus suggests this way to his disciples: He said to them, *"But now let the one who has a moneybag take it, and likewise a knapsack. And let the one who has no sword sell his cloak and buy one."*

Herein is exposed a mechanism of acquiring either money or a sword: sell what you have to obtain money and buy a sword. Money has always been the source of power. Whenever ancient cities dominated politics, these were also the wealthiest cities. That pattern is still maintained, though in a camouflaged way. Kings, emperors, governors, presidents, ministers and law-makers were and will always be the richest people in their countries, all organized around their respective government's politico-economic entities. The easiest way to make money two thousand years ago was to own the strongest military (sword). A strong military can invade an area and subjugate it, impose regulations and exploit its wealth. An army would also protect the riches it had already taken from the oppressed. As the best way to make money was to expropriate the resources of a particular land and protect those once owned, societies became organized around the military. Today's laws and regulations are knitted in such a manner to favor and protect the money-making mechanism of the rich under authoritarian military regimes. What we see being defined as democracy is just another form whereby everything we do is allowed as long as it does not infringe on the laws that favor and protect the rich people who control the country's resources. The remaining non-influential people are treated according to the judge's interpretation of the law. Today's rich people do not often pass as kings, emperors, presidents or governors; instead, they used their riches to appoint and dethrone governments that do not serve their interests through financing military conflicts around the globe like the one in my country, the Democratic Republic of Congo.

There cannot be much money without the sword or sword without money. They are to each other what life is to blood and blood to life: to acquire and protect.

Being a victim of an ethnic and financed military conflict, I came to a reasonable understanding that there cannot be a public mass spillage of human blood by another human being without political involvement, even in its primitive form. We have all heard people speak of psychopaths and sociopaths, who are simply morally depraved individuals, unstoppable and untreatable predators whose extreme violence is planned purposefully and remorselessly. When these people murder, we always analyze their perceptible characteristics. But let us look first at the meaning of the word *"politic"* that comes from the Latin word *"politicus"* meaning *"among others."* These "others" are referred to as civil servants or citizens. So politics is a process by which a group of people make collective decisions, but it also consists of "social relations involving authority or power" or plans of action used to create and apply principles. A psychopath converses with his desire, which is a talking serpent with all its other forms of energy, for a lengthy amount of time within his inner empire. After craftily processing his plan of action and deliberating on it and drawing what seems to him to be a policy line, the murder is committed with such an appetizing zeal as though the act itself was the greatest moral thing to do. This example is quoted here to enable your understanding to go beyond the words. The term *"by your sword you shall live"* might steer your intellect to western political powers that are predominately waging war in every corner of the globe under the pretext of peace and democracy and seemingly supporting the state of Israel. Or else you might think of the Jewish money to be the sign of the sword among them, or perhaps the Romans and Germans who historically committed indescribable crimes against the Jews in a rage that matched that of Esau's descendants. The truth, however, is that these cannot be specific countries and their governments because the concept of the world politico-economic power is built on a collective desire of some filthy rich mighty individuals hidden behind hierarchical or class-conscious social organizations (governments) that are used as apparatuses (talking serpents) to carry out their sinister essence. These class-conscious people are those who are of the same spirit as those at the tower of Babel. The ungodly thought that man could understand the world through his activities. At the same time, being aware of the confusion of thoughts (languages) brought about by God to awaken man's consciousness of Him, they are currently using wars (Esau's sword) to steer the already suffering human spirit to their original desire of a world without God. They know that if man is subjected to much suffering he will end up denying God's existence as I did in my childhood (reference to Job's wife in the book of Job). On the other hand, Israel being the pivot point, there is a great motivation to serve him with the sword (money) in order to get closer and control him, but the latter does not weary of the struggle between men and God. You might have wondered where the Jewish money comes from. Some of us thought it was God's providence to his chosen nation; of course it is God's providence to have Esau's sword serve his brother Jacob ("Israel") but for how long?

The Bible answers: *"when you grow restless, you shall break his yoke from your neck."* Many view this passage as though it will be the emancipation of Esau from the curse of being a servant to his brother Jacob. A man of the sword is capable of freeing himself at any given time, as long as his goal of freedom is achieved and this of course cannot be achieved peacefully. He is in that position of servitude because he desired to be and thought it to be a better position to achieve his desire. But when he realizes that he is going nowhere and that nothing is achieved through desire that has been cursed to crawl on its belly, he will definitely try to use his sword to free himself by slashing the yoke that is always by nature disturbing. This war-like attitude would be an attempt to change the entire plan of human salvation, and the whole human race would be at risk if Israel's survival was jeopardized.

As we had seen above, actions are substantiated thoughts. This means that outside and within the very borders of Israel, there will be found people who are supportive of Esau's destructive spirit and motivated by their selfish desire to build an empire that does not recognize God.

Isaiah 14:12 -22 describes it clearly as the original thought (the son of Dawn)...who said in his heart (desire), "I will ascend to heaven 'by *building the Tower of Babel that reach heaven'* make a name for myself "*I will make myself like God.*" This is the original desire of Adam and Eve, of those at the tower of Babel and throughout all our generation with Esau's descendants who embodied the serpent of desire's nature by disguising themselves behind changing empires. But the Lord Almighty saw it all, and through his amazing grace, provision for our salvation was made possible. Isaiah 14:24 says:

> "*The Lord of hosts has sworn: As I have planned, so shall it be and as I have purposed, so shall it stand...*"

Chapter 14

The Essence of Atonement

Atonement is a noun that takes its root from the verb "cover" or an act that provides protection. We first saw at the end of chapter 7 how Adam and Eve tried to do this by covering themselves with fig leaves. In Judaism, atonement may occur through some form of repentance, confession, temple service such as bringing a sacrifice, which is not possible today, trials or afflictions (awful life experiences). As a final point death was the ultimate atonement with energy capable of covering not just people's sins, but also of restoring the land: Numbers 35: 33

> "You shall not pollute the land in which you live, for blood pollutes the land, and no atonement can be made for the land for the blood that is shed in it, except by the blood of the one who shed it."

It is from this principle of atonement that the pertinent philosophical principle of inter-relation of opposite forces derived. Philosophers believe that it is through the negation of the old that the new is born and that destruction is the mother of emergence. Only a perfect conscious destruction can be the mother of emergence because it is cognizant of the pathway that is taken by the energy released by the applied destruction, as well as its short and long term results. But we have seen that man is no longer a perfect conscious individual, so to put the power of destruction in his hands is an act that leads to the complete annihilation of the human race. Atonement was a provision that God put in place in order to keep his presence permanently before the Israelis as He led them around the world to proclaim his Name. It was introduced to Abraham when God asked him to sacrifice his only son, Isaac. This provision consisted in most cases of slaughtering an animal that was created like us in terms of dust and breath and that still listens without complaint to God's voice as put inside it: "instinct."

The Lamb was the animal considered most fit for such an act of Atonement. But there were times when such sacrifices did not work, due to the severity of the sin. Moses was the greatest and first prophet among the sons of Israel, yet because he failed to uplift the name of God in front of the people, he was punished by not being able to enter the Promised Land. Nothing sacrificial was worthy to be offered for atonement: Deuteronomy 32:49-52 says:

> "Go up this mountain of the Abarim, Mount Nebo, which is in the land of Moab, opposite Jericho, and view the land of Canaan, which I am giving to the people of Israel for a possession. 50 And die on the mountain which you go up, and be gathered to your people, as Aaron your brother died in Mount Hor and was gathered to his people, 51 because you broke faith with me in the midst of the people of Israel at the waters of Meribah-kadesh, in the wilderness of Zin, and because you did not treat me as holy in the midst of the people of Israel. 52 For you shall see

> the land before you, but you shall not go there, into the land that I am giving to the people of Israel."

In 1 Samuel 3: 14, Eli's house of iniquity was unforgiveable through sacrifices or offerings; death was the ultimate atonement. This means that at "certain death," man pays for his sins. The fact is that he pays for his sins by losing his essence, thus his life.

In fighting with God, the Israelites committed severe sins, and most of them were related to idolatry, which is a cult of images made by man through his activities and, as activated by his ego.

In a prophecy concerning Jerusalem, a city of much religious significance, Isaiah 22:14 wrote:

"The Lord of host has revealed Himself in my ears: Surely this iniquity will not be atoned for you until you die." Another translation says: *"until the day you die."* Either way this was a precarious situation because Jerusalem (Zion) was a city that was destined to be the worshiping place of our God forever, as stated in Psalms 48:8 *"....In the city of our God, which God will establish forever."* Death was the only remedial way to atone for Israel's iniquity.

Yet in Isaiah 43:24-25 it says: *"You have not brought me sweet cane with money, or satisfied me with the fat of your sacrifices. But you have burdened me with your sins; you have wearied me with your iniquities. 25 I, I am He who blots out your transgressions for my own sake, and I will not remember your sins."*

So in verse twenty-five, the Lord God reveals that He alone can blot out Israelite's transgressions so that they will not die. But the question arises, how is that possible? Definitely as it says in verse 24 of Him being burdened with Israel's sin, Isaiah was trying to give us a mental picture of God carrying those sins on His shoulders and enduring their ultimate consequence, which was death as it was promised to Jerusalem in the prophecy of Isaiah 22: 14. This alone is the ultimate revelation of the greatest love of God. How could such an amazing infinite God endure the consequences of Israel's sin and die in their place so that the whole world could be saved? How could this be possible? It is through the coming of the Messiah, *"the anointed."*

Chapter 15

The Essence of the Messiah

Millions of Jews around the world are still waiting for the coming of the Messiah, *"The anointed one of Israel."* They have spent millennia praying for His coming through their daily sanctification of God's name *"Hashem."* There is a reason that they are still doing this, and it is based on an expectation described in the following Bible scripture: Isaiah 2:1-4 says,

> *"¹ The word that Isaiah the son of Amoz saw concerning Judah and Jerusalem. Now it will come about that in the last days, the mountain of the house of the Lord will be established as the chief of the mountains, and will be raised above the hills; and all the nations will stream to it.*
>
> *³ And many peoples will come and say, 'come, let us go up to the mountain of the Lord, to the house of the God of Jacob; that He may teach us concerning His ways and that we may walk in His paths.'*

> *For the law will go forth from Zion*
> *and the word of the Lord from Jerusalem.*
>
> *⁴ And He will judge between the nations,*
> *and will render decisions for many peoples;*
> *and they will hammer their swords into plowshares and their*
> *spears into pruning hooks.*
>
> *Nation will not lift up sword against nation,*
> *and never again will they learn war."*

It is true and certain that Israel will be restored at the coming of the Messiah, and they will be gathered back home from exile; the Messiah will be from the house of David, and the purpose of His coming will be to restore Israel eternal life.

But one rule is skipped here: there can never be forgiveness of sin without atonement, and in this case it was the death of Israel as referred to in the prophecy above about Jerusalem.

But The Lord God volunteered as seen in Isaiah 43:24-25 *"I, I am He who blots out your transgressions for my own sake, and I will not remember your sins."*

This shows how far the Lord went to save Israel and to save the gentiles as well.

In most cases, whenever there was a sin that was afflicting the nation, salvation was only possible if the sinner is found, judged and punished, or a sacrifice equal to the sin was offered, thus rendering it redemptive. In Israel's case his sin was redemptive only through his death. There were no other alternative means of redemption to blot out its sin if not God Himself. We have to know that Israel's exile and afflictions were just consequences of its sin, which cannot be atoned only worsened. It is only through a set sacrifice that sin can be atoned, *not through its consequences.* There is a difference between paying for one's action and enduring its consequences. Payment is the fixed price or sentence decreed for breaking the law, while consequences are effects of the act resulting dependently and independently from both the act and the punishment allotted to it, but not limited by them. For example, to falsely testify to a jury in a court of law is a perjury. Based on this act alone, we can be convicted or fined within the provision of the law. If the sentence is carried out or fined paid, we may say that we have paid the full price of breaking the law by committing perjury. But in a next court session with a different case to testify in front of the same presiding jury, it will be difficult to prove to a jury that has lost trust in us in the previous court case that we are telling the truth. They may simply disqualify us as potential witness, and this lack of the jury trusting us may be referred to as one of the consequences of committing the first offence of perjury.

The consequences of sin can also alter our chemical and physical composition completely and result in our death even when we have already paid a lesser price than death as fixed by the law. It is now clear why death is called the ultimate price; with it, everything ends. So when you see someone going through hardships, you should not use the expression: "*He is paying for his sins*," instead say, "*He is afflicted by his sins.*"

How could God be among men to die for their sins and still spare their lives? According to Exodus 33:20 is it not recorded: "*You cannot see my face, for man shall not see me and live.*" The answer lies in the fact that God, being Existence and the Creator of everything, is capable of tapping into his conscious energy and reproducing a physical "form" of Himself to carry out the purpose needed for atonement.

Due to the perfect nature of this physical form and its purpose, a well-defined trajectory which was conducive to such perfection was used: a virgin had to become pregnant without any sexual act involved.

This process is also at the same time a great revelation to us in the fact that the first Adam, as we saw him prior to requesting a partner, was endowed with the quality of reproducing without *a separate* female counterpart. He possessed that ability to procreate himself.

Abraham and Sarah were biologically too old to have a child but it is known that Sarah conceived at ninety years of age though "the way of women," as the Bible said it, had ceased to be with her. A miracle occurred, because they probably did not sleep together with an intention to conceive a child due to the fact that a sexual act itself was useless for that purpose. Now that we understand how God deals sometimes with those He blesses, can we claim Jesus Christ to be from David's bloodline without Joseph taking part in Mary's pregnancy? Yes we can if we can say that Isaac was Abraham's son. To every Jew who denies that Jesus Christ is not from David's lineage, let it be said to him that Abraham likewise is not his ancestor, because Isaac, who fathered Israel (Jacob) was not conceived sexually in the conventional way due to the advanced age of both his parents. If Isaac miraculously carried Abraham's blood in his veins, so is Jesus Christ the son of David. Jesus was God made in human form to die for Israel's sins and so pave the way to salvation, which was already in jeopardy for all people. His death benefited the Gentiles, whose lives depended on the Jews who could not carry their given mission due to transgressions. At some point, man may wonder why God had to do it this way. It is as if God does not have the power to overcome His own indignation over the rebelliousness of creation except by sacrificing His Son, knowing full well that this will save the souls of all believers, past, present and future, even though the rebellion continues today. Is this act itself irreverent? No, it is an act of divine wisdom and love that transcends our understanding. God is cognizant of all events and actions and he knew perfectly and chose a better way to make us completely humble once confronted with the essence of Christ. Christ, as God made flesh, endured all types of human tribulations, and was denied by his own to finally die a cruel death on a cross. Only God could have done this. Islam and Judaism always defy who Jesus Christ truly was. The message is now simple: He was a form of God made flesh to accomplish His restorative mission through His death so that we can be saved. This essence persisted throughout His life here on earth as Jesus Christ (name in the essence). Once He died His mission was complete and His energy returned to God, from whence it came. When Peter wrote of the resurrection of Jesus Christ, he said of Him in 1 Peter 3:22: *"…who has gone into heaven and is at the right hand of God."*

If we consider Isaiah 63:5, which says: *"therefore my own arm brought salvation for me,"* you will discover that God's hand is used most often to embody an action of service. It is Him alone or His hand alone that avenges Him because there is no one else who can match His power for salvation.

The fact that Jesus Christ, the essence of the Anointed One, the Messiah, takes His place at the right hand of God symbolizes that the hand is still in position of service, and It might be needed anytime to perform another act of wonder as we all are still expecting in the second coming, when Christ will be revealed as Lord of All, our conquering King. The reality is that the Jews, who were supposed to be the primary beneficiaries of this act of sacrifice that had both potential chemical and physical reactants to activate the survival of the human race, denied it; and furthermore, they rejected Him who carried the restorative essence. This conduct itself could have meant our total destruction. But instead their rejection of the Messiah later gave birth to our belief thus saved us as Gentiles. We, the Gentiles, believe in Him and recognize His essence.

A believer is not someone who embraces beliefs blindly without scrutinizing them as most people define Him or have a tendency to use the word "believer" in that way. A believer instead is someone who took the time to analyze facts that are "rejected" by some and on them built on his conviction that they are true. It is through enduring convictions that Faith is built. A faith without convictions is not faith. There would be no word "belief" if there were no doubt, denial or rejection in the world of thought. Now that our beliefs as non-Jews (Gentiles) are considered suitable for our salvation—which should not have been the case if the Jews did accept Jesus—God's act of accepting our faith was called "*Grace*," which is defined as an undeserved gift.

So let us be wise never to look down on the Jews because of their denial of Christ. Their attitude to Christ should be a reminder to us of how blessed we are today to be able to spend eternity with the God of Abraham, Isaac and Jacob. What our mission as Christians should be is to support Israel throughout their struggle rather than judging them lest we end up offering a helping hand to Esau, who holds the sword. Let us identify Israel as a resilient nation that has played both undeniable destructive and constructive roles in the restoration of God's oneness with mankind. It is not mere randomness that the controversial figure of the state of Israel dominates our modern world as its legitimate foundation was in 1948; this is its true essence as recorded through the annals of old, particularly in the Bible itself. We should never underestimate an attitude that saved our lives, because therein lies a mystery of what we are today. Romans 11:25-36 says: "*Lest you be wise in your own sight, I want you to understand this mystery, brother; a partial hardening has come upon Israel, until the fullness of the Gentiles has come in. 26 And in this way all Israel will be saved, as it is written,*

'The Deliverer will come from Zion,
he will banish ungodliness from Jacob;

27 and this will be my covenant with them
when I take away their sins.'

28 As regards to the Gospel, they are enemies of God for your sake. But as regards to election, they are beloved for the sake of their forefathers. 29 For the gifts and the calling of God are irrevocable. 30 For just as you were at one time disobedient to God but now have received mercy because of their disobedience, 31 so they too have now been disobedient in order that by the mercy shown to you they also may now receive mercy. 32 For God has consigned all to disobedience, that he may have mercy on all.

33 Oh, the depth of the riches and wisdom and knowledge of God! How unsearchable are his judgments and how inscrutable his ways!

34 'For who has known the mind of the Lord,
or who has been His counselor?'

35 'Or who has given a gift to Him
that He might be repaid?'

36 For from Him and through Him and to Him are all things. To Him be glory forever. Amen."

Chapter 16

Success Versus Our Reality

We have just seen how our reality is unpredictable because of our unfamiliarity with the fusion of our behavioral energy (thoughts or actions) with the outside world. We also saw how it all started with the first man in the Garden of Eden, with those at the tower of Babel, with Abraham, Jacob (Israel) and Esau who is currently embodied by individuals behind the authoritative body of governments that rule the world. We also finally saw the essence of Jesus Christ, His death and its inclusive grace for Gentiles.

Now the biggest question remains: how can we still be successful in everything we do while living in this uncertain world? How can we still achieve or secure pious productivity while being ambivalent about what our behavioral energy will yield for us?

It is not by chance that I chose the word "success," which I consider to be the cradle of both happiness and sadness. A friend of mine always wanted to know the reason why I describe success to be the cradle of two opposite elements. My answer is that the level of every good thing is not only measured by the depth of its goodness but also by its endurance to keep itself good when harshly challenged. It is our misuse of good that creates or substantiates what is bad. The fact is that everything good is by itself a stimulus (energy composition) with its own properties or configurations that derived from the original infinite constant energy (God's consciousness). These combined properties embody their antithesis, which can surge if the law that sustains them is trifled with. If you can think of anything bad, it will always lead you to where the law was broken from what was good to become that which is called "bad." Even murder committed by a close friend can be traced to a severe hatred that was born out of those good years of passionate love that became an obsession, so that the result is murder.

When God created the universe all things in it were "good." It is man who tempted with their energy compositions, which are chemical, brought out their dormant antithesis.

What does success mean to you? Everybody has his own views. For many people, success is to always get what they want. Yes, as mentioned before, the word success is truly the cradle of happiness and sadness because it is the fiber through which our single activity is defined, based on our intentions and expectations. Success can come in both constructive and destructive ways depending upon our intentions and the way we conceive them. What would you have to be doing to feel successful? Many will answer: to have a good career, to make more money so that I can donate to more charities, to afford anything at any time that I need and so on. There is a long list of goals that make well-intentioned people feel successful. But the ill-intentioned, as defined by moral individuals, do not consider themselves to be bad at all—they will say for example that their list of goals includes: seeing every Christian slaughtered, or eliminating the entire race. The list is long, and it would make them feel successful if these things were achieved.

In both cases, the intentions have different mental objects, but these goal-oriented objects produce the same feeling of satisfaction in two different individuals, namely the feeling of being successful. Why is this so?

The answer is that, in both illustrations, man satisfies his desire, and desires are good when satisfied. But what does this make us? Obviously it makes us self-centered people who direct all of our attention of our intentions to ourselves. You read me right, attention of our intentions because our intentions need to be "focused" on the object of its interest also called center of interest before being substantiated. When we focus the whole attention of our thoughts only on our activities, we then devote ourselves excessively to the object of our intentions and become idolaters through our total devotion to our own activities, as found at the time of the tower of Babel. Some of you might be wondering: "how can I be an idolater when sometimes the object of my intention is for universal good?" The truth is that every intention is a prayer that navigates through our ecosystem to attract the object that aligns itself with our desire. You might be wondering yourself what difference is there between an intention and a desire? An intention is the plan of action to achieve your goals, purposes plus the motifs behind those goals, while a desire is to want anything strongly and it always precedes our intentions. For example: you may desire to have money which is not bad in itself and this feeling grips us by the fact that we observe how money gives freedom to those who have it. By the time our desire engages our mind only in forming a plan of action to get to the desired object for the purpose of acquiring the desired freedom and then the mind anticipates our plan of action—a role that our conscience must play—right there it becomes an intention (a prayer based purely on a desire).

Our intention is the link between our desire and its goals. Our attention is born through our senses, which are the windows through which we perceive the outside world. To have someone pay attention is not to get him interested. We become interested when we consciously react positively or negatively to the impulse of our senses. A desire is born once we identify the essence of the object of our interest as related to our needs. After that, our intentions, which are the thoughts behind our needs, come in (why do we want it?) then the final execution. These methods are the AIDIA of every man's action: attention, interest, desire, intention, action. To whom do you pray every day? Who is your God? Definitely you did not know that by merely having an intention with regard to material things, you were praying to them to gratify your desire. Unfortunately, we cannot live in this world without having intentions about things we dearly want. Not all intentions are bad; we all need them to trigger our reality. But there is more to intentions than just the goals that we want to meet. Our intentions are the blueprint of our judgment. It is what we intend to do that is of paramount importance in deciding the nature of our desire. What about our actions, do they have any effect at all? I know some of us are guided by or have heard of Machiavelli's principle that "the ends justify the means."

In this philosophy everything is permissible as long as the ultimate outcome is good. This principle disguises the true essence of success in such a way that it leads many people who depend upon it astray. It states that evil is acceptable if it results in a greater good. Let us say that the genocide of a given nation result in permanent world peace. This is not acceptable. But is it the same if I see someone working on a weapon of mass destruction with the intention to eradicate the same nation. Am I morally bound to respect the person's choice and allow this evil so that good may come of it?

In philosophy, success is not measured by our reaction to an action, our career achievement, our material possession, or even through our intentions or accomplishments. Instead, success is measured by the "amount" of energy vested in our struggle to achieve a "good" intention (prayer), despite being confronted by the harshest challenges. From this definition you probably find that you have vested a lot of energy in a positive goal and ended up failing to achieve it, but still unsuspectingly achieve success. For example, an able man and a disabled man may be asked to climb twenty-five stairs in two minutes. If success needs to be awarded, it will definitely be given to the disabled man who achieved the highest calories burnt in just a quarter of a minute by climbing only five of the twenty-five stairs by the time the able guy had reached the stairs' top. Yet the question is still to be asked: how can we recognize surely that every aspect of our intended action is "good?" Many are those who will respond: by their end result, a response that gave shape to the saying "the ends justify the means."

As previously mentioned, human beings' current essence is not eternal—but his existence is eternal—because after the sin of Adam and Eve, our essence became chemically and physically ephemeral. Thus, we cannot understand the end result of any single action, even if during our life the results seemed always to be good. What is good and what is bad in our lives is but a sequence of our energy input (action) that takes its course until the end of time, which is unknowable. Ecclesiastes 6:12: *"For who knows what is good for a person in life, during the few and meaningless days they pass through like a shadow? Who can tell them what will happen under the sun after they are gone?"*

What has saved lives today may annihilate them tomorrow, today's good decision may turn disastrous a hundred years from now, and yesterday's nutrient may be today's lethal poison. What is intelligent education today may be unveiled as blatant ignorance in ten years.

Such is the course of our actions. Hence what we enjoy or dislike as a result of our good and bad deeds is but a flash of an ever-transforming force with *"unknown ends"* weaved in such a way that its chemical and physical composition aligns itself with our history and present actions, our location, climate or any other factor. The forces of past that led to who we are today, our environment, people we encounter might be symmetrical chemically and physically opposed to what we want to be or do in the future. This is the reason why we see evil happening to a good man or good happening to an evil man. Unexpected circumstances befall everyone. It is our striving to do what is good without recourse to bad means, no matter the consequences, that will be considered to be true success.

To be involved in any act of annihilation with the intent to correct an undesirable situation is to usurp God's role as the supreme Judge of the universe, Who genuinely knows what end truly justifies the means.

Having been a victim of political vilification, and beheld a close friend murdered, I often analyzed some cases such as that of the conviction of a serial killer, which can be viewed as a means to achieve a peaceful murder-free society which is a good end in itself. But this end, though achieved, might produce another reality in the community. For example, a rebel was arrested for carrying out the assassination of several high-profile African politicians. He was condemned to death in a military court for the murder of eight of them. During the trial, a list of those he killed and other targets to be killed was read in the court as one of the pieces of evidence against him. Among the names read was that of a politician who was to be the next victim when the rebel was caught. The government, in connivance with its military tribunal court, ordered the public execution of the rebel, and for the next few years no politician was afraid of being ambushed and murdered by a dissident. But as years passed, a successful military coup was launched against the government in place, and the president was overthrown and killed. As the shocked population watched and waited to see the man behind the upheaval, it realized that the politician who had been next on the rebel's murder list during the trial was the master mind behind the coup. If the rebel had not been arrested and convicted, the government and its president would have governed peacefully until the upcoming term. But due to a single decision made in the past that was viewed to be impeccably rational, the whole country was plunged into total chaos perpetrated by a cruel dictator. Through the above example we should understand that we cannot always anticipate a good outcome even if we try our best. We all must strive to do what is good regardless the outcome.

A man who confronts nation X peacefully without annihilating it from the map may save millions of lives. Sometimes peace cannot be achieved through nonviolence and many people may still lose their lives, but it is still and will remain the greatest energy ever vested rather than destroying the nation X in the name of peace. To allow evil that good may come of it through someone's choice to kill nation X is tantamount to doing it ourselves. What about evil committed in self-defense or other choices, like choosing one of your loved ones to die with you if forced by a killer who might choose more than one if you refuse to do what he demands? The answer to these questions fall into two categories: A self-defense theory is applied when a person is trapped in a situation brought about by an attacker who might severely harm or kill him. It is his maneuver to get out of the situation unharmed and alive that will be considered self-defense. As you are struggling with your foes, there might be a combination of unconscious moves and intentional one that might lead to the death of your opponents. It is these unconscious and intentional actions that were committed not with the purpose of causing harm or death to your opponent that will spare you from being a culprit in assault or murder charges. But any intentional moves will be judged by God who knows the combination of all actions. For example in the case of King David, whose hands were stained with blood from the wars fought for Israel, he was not allowed to build a temple for God.

Michael Halfom, a friend of mine, whom it is a great privilege to mention in this book, asked me on one occasion: "Why did God allow Adam and Eve's choice knowing that their action would plunge this world into chaos?

The answer is that stripping someone's choice is to enslave him completely and it was not God's intention to enslave human beings, but to offer them free will. However, to foresee that their choice would separate man from Him and still allow it, is another proof that the first man truly misused God's given freedom of choice purposely as an insult to His Spirit and a declaration of war for supremacy: Adam decided to wage a war he could not win against his Creator.

God knew that He could never be mistaken by allowing our freedom of choice, and He also knew that man would disobey Him but he wanted to walk him through a journey that would humble him as He did with me through my childhood. We are all put into an individually framed fate and it is the way in which we invest our energy to fight and surmount challenges that counts the most. Our intention should be to strive with our maximum energy to always do good even when it is not in our best interest and it is through that spirit of riding above the boisterous waves of circumstances that our efforts will be crowned "success."

Our intentions being prayers should be aligned with the constant energy capable of navigating us to our desired object. This constant energy is God, the One who does not change. Our intention's energy should fuse with the constant energy of God to create the object of our intention. Most people with whom I had time to share my experiences always asked me why God takes time to grant our desire while the "Devil" acts fast. First of all it must be understood that someone Who is not defined by time cannot be judged by it. There is no early or late for Him because anytime is always on time for our God. With that knowledge in mind you will come to the understanding that God provides even when you do not receive the object of your desire in this life. This is the reason why it seems like ages due to the fact that we, as humans, are the ones defined by time. We have seen who the Devil is and to answer the question of why he acts swiftly is: He only wants to convey one message: *"There is no other God, you are yourself through your intention born out of your desire."*

We saw that everything has its appropriate form of energy, and we can use it to reproduce matter or anything that we need if we align our thoughts with the object of our intention but with one rule "by the will of our God," Who knows the material composition of the object of our intention and the best point in time for its provisional manifestation.

Our environment, location, and energy flow at the time of our need for an object might produce a lethal formula that can totally disintegrate our essence and lead us to a kind of death. What is advised instead is to be focus on the ends through our dependency on God Who provides the rightful means at the right time for the right results that suit your current being's composition. Once again, the end does not justify the means; instead the end should be a merit acquired through rightful means that emanated from right intentions. Christians should be very cautious with the teachings of the law of attraction that promote a cult of self-worship (we are our own creators and we can get all that we need or want.)

In Matthew 7:7-11, Jesus said: "*Ask, and it will be given to you; seek, and you will find; knock and it will be opened to you. 8 For everyone who asks, he receives, and the one who seeks, he finds, and to the one who knocks it will be opened. 9 Or which one of you, if his son asks him for bread, will give him a stone? 10 Or if he asks for a fish, will give him a serpent? 11 If you then, who are evil, know how to give good gifts to your children, how much more will your Father who is in heaven give good things to those who ask him.*"

In this Biblical scripture Jesus said it well; to ask, not to get it by ourselves, to knock and not to enter without permission; between these suggestions he says to "*seek you will find.*" Through asking for an object, a person recognizes that he has no direct link to it if not through the provider's will to give. The same is applied to access, by knocking at the door we acknowledge it is not our own place, that we are not the "*Dominus*"—Master of the house or Owner. What we have on our side is our "*willingness and persistence,*" that is expressed here by the verbs "to ask," "to seek" and "knock." It is this attitude of *willingness* to do what is good while depending on the Lord *constantly* that can set us on the road to success. The recognition of God as the sole provider of everything through our intentions is a powerful weapon to fight our Desire. This being said, the book of Proverbs states it clearly in Chapter 3:5-6: "*Trust in the Lord with all your heart, and do not lean on your own understanding. 6 In all your ways acknowledge him, and he will make straight your paths*"

The ability to trust in the Lord must be accompanied by humility. Humility comes from the Latin word "*humilitas*" which means "low." Humility is that flexibility to relate to everyone else at their level while still maintaining ours, thus accepting them as who they are. It is that flexibility to fuse with other forms of energy while still maintaining control of our own. Humility has nothing to do with people with low self-esteem but with those with a high self-esteem, an attitude which is causal of ego, the life blood of desire. For a person with a high sense of self-esteem, the move to lower himself to the same level as anyone else might be considered as a loss of dignity instead of a reflex that inspires us with a servant's heart. To be humble is to embark on the road of compliance in order to blend together with any necessary force of lesser energy and with it, soar high. Without humility as one of the natural laws, there will be no flexibility or fluidity, but instead more pain. Our bones will not mend once broken and our heart will stop because the blood will not surrender to its pumping force. Humility allows our bodies to adapt to changes of our environment. It is this ability to react correctly to changes of nature that characterizes the law of humility and transforms us into heroes of survival.

However, humility does not mean that we should not be critical of the forms of energy blending with our own by being gullible, instead we need to cultivate an attitude of resilience. This attitude acknowledges that the one thing a person can know is what he does not know. In the pursuit of knowledge and truth, a person ought to demonstrate both sensitivity to the views of others and critical inquiry. Another way to express this is that the person with "*Socratic humility*" understands that anything can be questioned but at the same time that its essence need to be penetrated in order to achieve oneness with the object. Ego can erect a solid wall of presumptuousness around us but when a much stronger force collides with this wall it will crack or be broken in pieces because of its rigidity. By embracing challenges through penetration of their essence we end up achieving oneness with them, and then detachment.

In one of the laws of nature there is a system known by most economists: "the law of diminishing returns." If one input in the production of a commodity is increased while all other inputs are held fixed, a point will eventually be reached at which additions of the input yield progressively smaller, or diminishing, increases in output. For example, five people are needed to produce twenty bags of corn meal in a day. Adding more people for production while the farm maintains the same acreage, will cause production per person to decrease and that can affect the company. The more you eat something that tastes good, the less palatable it becomes.

The first time you experience pain generated by any of your circumstances, its force almost knocks you down. These circumstances can be the loss of a job, financial instability, loss of a loved one, or any painful emotion besieging our heart. It is written on every page of nature that the more the pain visits you, the less hostile it will be. Once you learn to embrace it as it comes, you will for eternity use its energy to work wonders while waiting on your Maker to reward you for your merit. We cannot talk of learning from hardship as making good come from evil. The difference is that hardships or suffering are circumstances befalling us caused by the fusion of our uncontrolled behavioral energy with other forms of energy in our cosmos, while evil is the immediate content of our action that has a negative effect on our survival. It is this immediate evil action and the intention behind it that people should not use as an excuse to try to make good come of it. Suffering can seem to result from evil but its influence on us can itself be redemptive. This process can be very painful but remember that true success in life usually comes with pain, and there will always be a sweet side to every pain.

Man is the only one at the center of all his calamities, having taken hold of the prohibited energy, an action triggered by his desire to equal God. The entire course of history since then has been guided by this energy that completely disintegrates his essence, or kills him through his own actions. So said, our reality is the result of our own conditioned situations, and the way we react to these situations is what matters the most in determining our future. We have to stop blaming a third party that we call "Satan," because Satan is man's own desire. In all the Bible narrations of the Children of Israel, God never condemned a personality named Satan if not the desire itself in them—the energy opposite to man's essence. The center of condemnation in the Bible has been totally focused on human beings, their actions and reactions to situations that are brought forth by their own intentions. The book of Job is the only place in the Holy Bible where God, who can communicate with anything, knowing that everything is living energy, speaks to the desire within man as an independent force to challenge Job's integrity. Simply put, there were already in Job a pride of self-sufficiency and independence. God conversing with Satan is God talking to Job's desire within him or to the Job within who was too proud. For all his life Job had enjoyed tremendous riches and blessings from God. He had never been exposed to misery because his entire composition at that specific location made it almost impossible for him to experience suffering. God knew Job's capability for endurance but the Job within was not so sure. That is why God allowed him to taste the consequences of his actions so that he could witness the disintegration of his own essence. This was the greatest challenge ever undertaken by a purely human being apart from Jesus who was God himself in the form of man. Job was humiliated and made ready to digest the lesson. After a series of questions filled with much wisdom and knowledge, Job confessed and repented. *"I know that you can do all things and no purpose of yours can be thwarted. Who is this that hides counsel without knowledge? Therefore I have uttered what I did not understand, things too wonderful for me, which I did not know. Hear, and I will speak; I will question you and you will make it known to me. I had heard of you by the hearing of the ears, but now my eyes see you; therefore I despise myself and repent in dust and ashes."* Job 42:2-6.

This was Job (the Job within) questioning God, and now that the Lord God answered him, he repented and experienced restoration beyond what he enjoyed before. We need to be humiliated, confess our sin and then repent in order to enjoy our restoration. As long as we are still proud of ourselves and feel self-sufficient in our activities we will always be humiliated through them, and this is the vanity of all vanities.

We have discovered that we were made with our unique life which contains a unique composition that will require a unique plan of action. We also learned that actions are, even at their primitive stage, an intention, and we finally concluded that our intentions are prayers. Now the question is: what are your prayers? What are your intentions? Is it to glorify yourself or your God?

Why do you truly need anything? Is it for you to satisfy your own desire (Bad) or it is for the satisfaction of your genuine desire to glorify your God from whom your entire essence comes (Good). Set your eyes on Jesus and the message of the Gospel, for who did He live for? Whose desire did He always put first? What was the essence of His death and His resurrection? It is only then that we can capture the true purpose of our lives here on earth and afterward. There are many Christians who think that they need to be baptized and then be born again and that is all. As far as I could meditate on this subject, I found out that to be born again does not mean to be baptized as others think. Let us think of the two thieves on the cross with Jesus dying next to them. Did one of them receive a baptism? The answer is no, but a promise was made to him that very day, so that he might find his place in heaven. So to be a real Christian, one does not necessarily need to be baptized. My uncle Martin that I called "father" was once baptized when he was a baby, but later on, he became an atheist. So we cannot be born Christians, but we become one by the second birth because of the Gospel that says—*"someone born, not from blood or from fleshly will or from man's will, but from God's." John 1: 13.* Our second birth is performed through God's will or desire to serve Him.

And you must know that each and every birth comes from a family. The physical birth in a physical family, the spiritual birth in a spiritual family and the latter is surely the Christian community like your respective churches. This Christian family is made up of men and women made new by this same experience. They have been completely changed by the power of the Gospel of Jesus Christ which is God's word and through it they were born again. The example of a butterfly can be most inspiring. A butterfly is an insect born twice. First, it lives as a caterpillar, then as a butterfly. This insect is able to go through a metamorphosis; this phenomenon changes the insect, its shape and its tastes. The leaves that were once its favorite foods are no longer important as they were when it was a caterpillar. But flowers and its pollens will be its delicious meals as a butterfly. We also undergo the same kind of metamorphosis, but in a spiritual way, when we encounter Jesus and accept Him in our hearts as our personal Savior. We are born again inwardly. We are made new. Our desire for sin, evil actions, drugs, alcohol, doubt, fear, hate no longer exists in us. Even if we are tempted we know how to transform that energy in our favor. We will not be stubborn or blind again. A kind of pure Energy will be activated; our persistence in doing what is bad as we were lacking a solution to life's difficulties extinguished this energy. This energy is our conscience, and it becomes pure and joy is restored immediately when we accept Christ. Our conscience will emerge in the form of an instinct or in a metaphysical way, to remind us that there is a God and that we need him to help us solve our problems, not that we are God and He does not exist.

Within our ever-changing global events, events from which we are not totally exempt, we must be true, to the very best that is within ourselves, while depending on the God of heaven and earth. We are God's army, honored to hold his divine authority. Our ignorance of this truth may easily lead us astray and make us miss things already in our divine purpose. We will finally end up complaining too much and question why our God gave us life?

One day as I was watching cars, a customer with his wife talked so decently to me that, seeing how kind they were, I was expecting a good tip. As the man fished into his pocket, he gave me a five cent coin of little or no value. I took courage to ask them if they knew how much they gave me. Surprised by my question, they took the coin from me and shouted at me, "You wouldn't have dared to ask us, because you don't even deserve the five cent coin and we are not indebted to give you anything."

This response made me think that if a simple human being is not obliged to give me a coin, how dare we complain to the Divine Infinity about why He created us, because we do not even deserve the least miserable life we live. He is not indebted to give us life the way we intend it to be. Let us not complain about things we are experiencing in our lives because the Almighty knows when on His divine calendar is the right time for any given event in our life according to our spiritual compositions.

Those of us who have embraced God during this earthly journey know by now from their blessed divine experience that He will not abandon them. As they trusted in Him on that ultimate day of their lives, they knew that it was the end of one mission and a preparation for an even greater one. This is the fact that sustained me, the truth that comforted me during my healing years; a certainty now embedded in my divine knowledge that guided me while I was bowed down with grief out of the shadows of dark clouds and into the light. How frail our life is! How predictable death is! We do not know when our chemical retrogression will reach its final stage by dissolving our current purpose of life. We must ask ourselves, "What are we going to do with our essence today, and how will this affect us tomorrow?" We probably have been conscience-smitten at a certain time of our lives for what we have done each day. But here are a few questions we should ask ourselves: "Have I done any good in the world today? Have I helped anyone in need including myself?" To have inspired gratitude in another human being and especially within ourselves can bring out the best within our human nature and transform the trajectory of our behavioral energy through our open ecosystem to a much more positive situation. By doing this we can easily and more clearly hear the laughter of our children, we can dry the tears of the weeping, and we can comfort the dying by sharing the promise of an eternal life. If we can lift one weary hand that hangs down, if we can comfort and bring peace to one struggling soul, if we can give as Jesus did, we can, by showing the way, become a guiding star for some lost sailors in our life's struggle, as Patrick Egboyo, Brad Eyre, Nancy, and Sarah did for me. And these lost sailors are our brothers, sisters, atheists and anyone out there who does not know the Lord. Some became so because of the unanswered questions to their misery. Life is fragile and death inevitable. We must make the most of each day, because there are many ways we can misuse our opportunities. May we resolve from now on to fill our hearts with love by going the extra mile to include in our lives anyone who is suffering, lonely or downhearted. May we cheer up the sad and make someone feel glad. May we live so that when we hear that final summons, we may have no guilt, or unfinished business, but be able to say with the Apostle Paul *"I have fought a good fight; I have finished my course..."* In other words, accomplished what my "essence" was required to accomplish: II Timothy 4:7.

Young men, now is the time to stand tall; do not get drained in filling your gap with God's knowledge, get answers to questions troubling you and use your given authority and energy to defeat Satan "your Youth Desire". If you know how to defeat him now, you will probably defeat him for a lifetime. Yes, at times you are snowed under by troubles, pains and grief, but you must not surrender to him, press on, go forward, smile at the fury of the storm and ride fearlessly and jubilantly across the boisterous ocean's waves of circumstances. Let the testimony of Jesus Christ, which is above mine and all others, light a lamp that will guide your vision through the portal of immortality, and communicate to your understanding the glory of God's knowledge. How I wish to look face to face into the eyes of all blessed readers and have them catch the energy of His knowledge through these words and truly understand who He is and what He is capable of accomplishing in your life. Enduring peace and security at some time in life should entice us to have a moment of reflection that will bring us to realize with surety that there is a God in heaven who is not a vengeful God with a million rules and harsh punishments, but a God Who has just one rule: to accept Him through love and obedience to his laws. He is simply kindness, gentleness and love, and He alone loves you. Seek strength from Him; He is in control and will help you, and that conviction alone is the core of a resilient reverence, and a chemical composition that can restore the true essence of our current reality.

GLOSSARY

Configurations: sub particles of any object with their individual role that were rearranged and gathered to give a mutual essence to another object.

Conscience: what we are asked to do by the moral law in order to keep some moral norms.

Conscientious consciousness: is consciousness based on the moral law.

Consciousness: the state of being mentally and physically aware of anything without any involvement with our conscience. Note: You can be conscious without being conscientious but you cannot be conscientious without being conscious.

Essence: an indispensable property of something that explains the reason of its being.

Matter: any substance that includes a mass and volume that is perceivable or imperceptible to our senses due to their limitation.

Paired reality: is a type of reality in which two different views complement each other in their truthfulness.

Transmutation: leaving one's original form in order to step into another entity's system and be that system with a mere purpose to attain a great deal of knowledge as how it functions.

Volitional state: is the power or faculty of choosing; the act or an instance of making a conscious choice or decision

ABOUT THE AUTHOR

 A law graduate from the University of Lubumbashi in Democratic Republic of Congo, Bosangs Dunn detains also a diploma in Latin Philosophy. Now an electronics assembler as well as a writer, he resides in Pennsylvania with his wife and two children.

CPSIA information can be obtained at www.ICGtesting.com
Printed in the USA
BVOW011530150812

297892BV00001B/10/P